THE EVERYTHING KIDS' LEARNING FRENCH BOOK

Fun exercises to help you learn *français*

DAWN-MICHELLE BAUDE, Ph.D.
Technical Review by VÉRONIQUE MOTERLÉ, Ph.D.

adamsmedia
Avon, Massachusetts

Special thanks for this book goes to a group of French kids, including Alba, Aleyna, Andrew, Axil, Arthur, Elise, Leonard, Leo, Louis, Noah, Shawn, Sophie and Theo, whose off-hand conversation supplied many case studies for this book. I would also like to thank my agent, Gina Panettieri, for her wisdom and patience in getting this book into print, and Kerry Smith at Adams Media for ensuring its quality. I would also like to thank Dr. Kyoko Inoue, for teaching me to how to think about grammar, and Sally Fischer, for outstanding support. And I especially want to thank my son Alex, for his meaningful insights into kids' French.

DIRECTOR OF INNOVATION Paula Munier

EDITORIAL DIRECTOR Laura M. Daly

EXECUTIVE EDITOR, SERIES BOOKS Brielle K. Matson

ASSOCIATE COPY CHIEF Sheila Zwiebel

ACQUISITIONS EDITOR Kerry Smith

DEVELOPMENT EDITOR Katie McDonough

PRODUCTION EDITOR Casey Ebert

An Everything® Series Book.
Everything® and everything.com® are registered trademarks of F+W Media, Inc.

Published by Adams Media, a division of F+W Media, Inc.
57 Littlefield Street, Avon, MA 02322. U.S.A.
www.adamsmedia.com

ISBN-10: 1-59869-543-6
ISBN-13: 978-1-59869-543-4

Printed by RR Donnelley, Harrisonburg, VA, USA

10 9

December 2014

Library of Congress Cataloging-in-Publication Data
is available from the publisher.

This publication is designed to provide accurate and authoritative information with regard to the subject matter covered. It is sold with the understanding that the publisher is not engaged in rendering legal, accounting, or other professional advice. If legal advice or other expert assistance is required, the services of a competent professional person should be sought.

—From a *Declaration of Principles* jointly adopted by a Committee of the American Bar Association and a Committee of Publishers and Associations

Many of the designations used by manufacturers and sellers to distinguish their products are claimed as trademarks. When those designations appear in this book and Adams Media was aware of a trademark claim, the designations have been printed with initial capital letters.

Cover illustrations by Dana Regan.
Interior illustrations by Kurt Dolber.
Puzzles by Scot Ritchie.

*This book is available at quantity discounts for bulk purchases.
For information, please call 1-800-289-0963.*

Visit the entire Everything® series at *www.everything.com*

CONTENTS

INTRODUCTION

**W**elcome to *The Everything® KIDS' Learning French Book!* This book is designed to help you learn French the fun way—using topics that are of interest to you, simple explanations, and exercises and games to test your skills.

Learning a new language is like opening a door to a whole new world. You step through that door, and discover new ideas, sights, and sounds. You learn about how other people live and think. The similarities among all peoples remind us how we're all very much alike, and the differences remind us that the world is a big, interesting place, just waiting to be discovered.

French kids are like kids anywhere—they go to school, play with friends, enjoy favorite foods, and watch movies. But they also have some things that make them different.

French kids are, well, *French*, which means they speak a language and live in a culture that is different in some ways from other languages and cultures. After school, they might put a bar of chocolate between two pieces of bread, and call it *pain-au-chocolat* ("chocolate bread"). American kids usually don't do that, but they might want to try it one day, since it's so good!

But no matter where they grow up, kids all around the world learn languages the same way. They begin with the alphabet and the numbers. Then they add vocabulary, one word at a time. "Hi," "please," "thank you," and "goodbye" are the first words to learn in any language. Little by little, the vocabulary begins to add up. Put a few words together, and you make a phrase. Eventually, you make full sentences. Before you know it, you're having a conversation.

Learning a language is a lot like playing with a building block toy. You have your favorite blocks, and you learn to arrange them. You might use the blocks to build a beautiful castle. Then you can take the castle apart and use the same blocks to build a huge hotel. Words work like that, too. You can use them in different ways to suit your purpose.

Take the verb, "to want," for example. In French it's *vouloir*. You may want ice cream. Or you may want louder music. Or you may want a new CD, a ticket to a movie, or... sleep! *Vouloir* is one of the first verbs you'll learn in this book, so you can tell someone what you want!

Having some building blocks is essential, but you also have to know how to put those blocks together. You don't want to build a castle that you have to hold up with both hands! You want it to stand up solidly on its own.

Using words to build sentences requires know-how. Grammar—the rules that hold language together—helps you use words in order to get the effect you want. You don't need to learn a lot of grammar rules to communicate clearly; you just need a few.

This book gives you the basics to get started. As you go on to study French, you'll continue to learn about the language so that you can build more elaborate sentences. The more French you understand, the more the door opens onto a new world. French is a very rich, complex language, full of surprises. It's also a fun language to learn and to speak.

So "let's get going." Or, as the French would say, *Allons-y!*

CHAPTER 1

Let's Get Started! —Allons-y!

Getting to Know French—
A la rencontre du français

You already know some French! Maybe you've had a chance to eat Brie, a French cheese? Or have you gone to a matinée? Do you know any brunettes? And you certainly know what dessert is, don't you? How about a chocolate éclair?

Some French words are so much a part of English that we don't think of them as French; we think of them as English. The two languages are old friends, after all. Both English and French partly grew out of an ancient language called Latin, spoken over two thousand years ago.

As English developed over the last 600 years, it borrowed a lot of words from French. Some of them, like "imagination," are so familiar it's hard to "imagine" they were ever French! But many English words that we use all the time have French origins.

Luckily, the shared words usually mean the same thing in both French and English. Here is a list of some you know:

- art
- ballet
- blond
- biscuit
- corduroy
- crayon
- denim
- dentist
- fruit
- mayonnaise
- menu
- niece
- omelet
- petite
- pioneer
- portrait
- rectangle
- restaurant
- somersault
- tennis
- trophy

Can you think of other words from French that we use in English? You know a lot more than you think you do!

The Alphabet—*L'alphabet*

You know the English alphabet, right? Then you know the French one, too! The letters are the same, but they work a little differently than they do in English. When you say the letters in French, you want them to sound like French. That

brunette

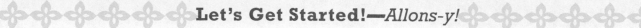

means you need to learn how to pronounce, or say, the letters the way French speakers do.

Most letters in French sound like their names. But some, such as the *w*, don't. Like the English name for "w" ("double-u"), the French *w* has a name that is different than it sounds. And some French letters have special marks, called "accents," that tell you how to pronounce the letter.

Letter	Name sounds like	Example
A	ah	*aller* (to go)
B	bay	*bébé* (baby)
C	say	*céréale* (cereal)
D	day	*décembre* (December)
E	er	*effacer* (erase)
F	eff	*fleur* (flower)
G	jay	*geyser* (geyser)
H	osh	*hauteur* (height)
I	e	*idée* (idea)
J	gee	*jouet* (toy)
K	ka	*kangourou* (kangaroo)
L	el	*miel* (honey)
M	em	*mouton* (sheep)
N	en	*nid* (nest)
O	oh	*olivier* (olive tree)
P	pay	*pélican* (pelican)
Q	kew	*queue* (tail)
R	air	*raton* (raccoon)
S	es	*santé* (health)
T	tay	*thé* (tea)
U	ew	*univers* (universe)
V	vay	*végétarien* (vegetarian)
W	DO-bluh-vay	*wagon* (train car)
X	eex	*xylophone* (xylophone)
Y	e-GRECK	*yaourt* (yogurt)
Z	zed	*zéro* (zero)

MISTAKES TO AVOID
Fautes à éviter

In French, the words all run together when we say them out loud. Making a link between sounds in a word or between words is called a "liaison." For example, *je ne sais pas* ("I don't know") really sounds like *jenesaispas*. When you speak French, try not to put too much of a pause between words.

Alphabackwards

le miel

le kangourou

le jouet

le bébé   aller

Somebody put the letters up backwards. Can you make out the French words here?

The French word for "mirror" is *miroir*.

*Hold the page up to the mirror to read the words.

Now that you know the French alphabet, you have to repeat it to learn it. Because the French alphabet has the same twenty-six letters as the English alphabet, you can recite the "alphabet song" you learned in kindergarten. Keep the same melody, but use the French pronunciation.

Essential Vocabulary—_Vocabulaire de base_

When you learn a new language, you learn words, or "vocabulary." Certain words you have to know right away, such as "yes," "no," and "hungry." They're the words you use all the time, over and over, every day. You say hi to people, ask for information, and answer questions. Here are some you need in French:

English	French	Pronunciation
Hi	_Salut_	SAH-loo
What's up?	_Ça va?_	SAH-vah?
Yes	_Oui_	We
No	_Non_	Noh
OK	_D'accord_	DA-core
Let's go	_On y va_	OHN-e-vah
Wait	_Attends_	AH-tahn
I'm hungry	_J'ai faim_	JAY-fah
What	_Quoi_	_Kwah_
I don't understand	_Je n'ai pas compris_	Jeh-NAY-paw-COHM-pree
Sorry	_Pardon_	PAHR-don
Repeat	_Répétez_	REH-peh-tay
Please	_S'il vous plaît_	SILL-vous play
Thank you	_Merci_	MARE-see
Bye	_A plus_	AH-ploos

J'ai faim!

After learning some basic words in a new language, it's time to put them together in sentences. In English, you put words together without even thinking about it. The same will be true for you in French.

Spelling and Pronunciation—
Orthographe et prononciation

Letters make all different kinds of sounds in different languages. As you learned to speak, you learned the sounds in English, just as French kids learned the sounds in French. Now you're going to learn which letters have the same sounds in both languages. You also need to learn a few new sounds.

Letter	In French sounds like...	Example
Aa	"a" in "ah"	*Amérique* (America)
Bb	"b" in "butter"	*bateau* (boat)
Cc	"k" in "kite"	*capitaine* (captain)
Dd	"d" in "dog"	*dame* (woman)
Ee	"a" in "about"	*dessin* (drawing)
Ff	"f" in "friend"	*fée* (fairy)
Gg	"g" in "game"	*galet* (pebble)
Hh	Often silent, as in "right"	*hamac* (hammock)
Ii	"e" as in "see"	*île* (island)
Jj	"j" as in "jump"	*jardin* (garden)
Kk	"k" as in "kite"	*kilo* (kilogram)
Ll	"l" as in "love"	*livre* (book)
Mm	"m" as in "mom"	*maman* (mom)
Nn	"n" as in "new"	*nuque* (back of neck)
Oo	"o" as in "octopus"	*objet* (object)
Pp	"p" as in "party"	*Pâques* (Easter)
Qq	"k" as in "kite"	*quiche* (cheese tart)
Rr	"r" as in "right"	*roue* (wheel)
Ss	"s" as in "sand"	*soleil* (sun)
Tt	"t" as in "television"	*tortue* (tortoise)
Uu	"oo" as in "oops"	*uniforme* (uniform)
Vv	"v" as in "valentine"	*vent* (wind)
Ww	"v" as in "valentine"	*wagon* (train car)
Xx	"x" as in "x-ray"	*xylophone* (xylophone)
Yy	"y" as in "yes"	*yaourt* (yogurt)
Zz	"z" as in "zebra"	*zéro* (zero)

Special Sounds—*Sons spéciaux*

You know how the "s" in the English word "sea" also makes a "z" sound in the English word "chose"? The same thing happens in French. A letter can make more than one sound, depending on the letters that are next to it.

Here are a few of these letters in French:

Letter	As In	Turns into	Example
c	"kite"	"s" as in "sand" after an "e" "a, "or "i"	*glace* (ice cream)
g	"game"	"dj" as in "measure" before an "e" or "i"	*genou* (knee)
l	"love"	"y" as in "yes" when followed by an "l"	*fille* (girl)
y	"yellow"	"e" as in "see" when it is alone	y (it, there)

Special Consonants—*Consonnes spéciales*

You probably learned at school that two consonants that melt together in a single sound are called "blends." The French blends are just like the English ones, with some exceptions.

Blend	As In	Turns into	Example
th	"thumb"	"t" as in "top"	*thé* (tea)
ch	"chain"	"sh" as in "ship"	*chanter* (sing)

And French has consonant blends we don't have in English at all! Here's one you should know:

Blend	Sounds like	Example
gn	"yn" in "canyon"	*vigne* (vine)

Special Vowels—*Voyelles spéciales*

French has a special group of vowels called "nasal vowels." They're called "nasals" because the sound they make is in your nose! These vowels are written different ways (*an, en, in, on, om, un*), but they all sound almost the same, like "aw" in the noise a donkey makes, "hee-haw"!

There are a few other vowel combinations you should know:

Combination	Sounds like	Example
eu	"ew"	*yeux* (eyes)
eur	"er" in "her"	*beurre* (butter)
oeur	"er" in "her"	*soeur* (sister)
au	"oh"	*chaud* (hot)
aux	"oh"	*chaux* (chalk)
eau	"oh"	*bateau* (boat)
eaux	"oh"	*ciseaux* (scissors)
ou	"boot"	*roue* (wheel)
our	"our" in "your"	*bonjour* (hello)

Adding Accents—*Mettre des accents*

French gets even more sounds out of the same letters by adding accents. Some, like the *accent circonflexe*, you'll like right away. Informally it's called the *chapeau* ("hat") in French, because French kids draw it over the letters the same way you draw a hat over a head in a picture you're making. Here are the accents and the jobs they do:

Accent	Name	Job	Example
^	*circonflexe*	tells us that a long time ago, there was another letter in the word that dropped out	*hôtel* (hotel)
Çç	*cédille*	changes the "k" sound to an "s" sound	*garçon* (boy)
´	*aigu*	makes the "e" sound like the vowel in "day"	*école* (school)
`	*grave*	makes the "e" sound like the vowel in "get"	*père* (father)
		makes the "a" sound similar to the vowel in "dad"	*là* (there)
¨	*tréma*	shows that two vowels are pronounced separately	*Noël* (Christmas)

Now let's see how you do. Look at the following words and pronounce each one carefully. Remember, the sound changes depending on the letters that are next to it. To help you out, the letter you need to pay attention to is in boldface type. Hint: The underlined letter in each line is pronounced differently in each word.

- <u>c</u>apitaine, gla<u>c</u>e, gar<u>ç</u>on
- <u>g</u>alet, <u>g</u>enou
- <u>y</u>aourt, <u>y</u>

- <u>d</u>essin, <u>é</u>cole, <u>p</u>ère
- <u>l</u>ivre, fi<u>ll</u>e

Now try to match the English sounds with the French sounds. See if you can answer the following questions:

1. Which French letter sounds like the "a" in "Dad"? _____

2. Which French letters sound like the "sh" in "ship"? _____

3. Which French letters sound like "oo" in "boot"? _____

4. Which French letter is often silent? _____

Numbers—*Les chiffres*

Knowing numbers in a new language is very important. How else can you ask for two pieces of pizza, or tell someone that there are twenty-one kids in your class? Since you already know how numbers work in English, you just have to learn their names in French. Here are the ones you need:

Numeral	French	Sounds Like
0	zéro	ZAY-roh
1	un	uh
2	deux	duh
3	trois	trwah
4	quatre	COT-truh
5	cinq	sank

> ## MISTAKES TO AVOID
> ### *Fautes à éviter*
>
> Not every letter in French is pronounced. A lot of them are silent. *Eau* ("water") has three vowels, but it's pronounced like "oh." And *ciseaux* ("scissors") is pronounced "SEE-zoh." Soon you'll get the knack for which letters need to sound and which are silent.

Funny Phone

Jacques is saying his phone number. But what language is that? He's not really speaking a language, but the sounds are right. Can you write the actual number beside the word? Try saying it out loud.

trwah ____

trwah ____

uh ____ sank ____

zayroh ____ set ____

weet ____ weet ____

duh ____ duh ____

nuhf ____

Numeral	French	Sounds Like
6	six	sees
7	sept	set
8	huit	weet
9	neuf	nuhf
10	dix	dees
11	onze	ohnz
12	douze	dooz
13	treize	trez
14	quatorze	KA-torz
15	quinze	kanz
16	seize	says
17	dix-sept	DEE-set
18	dix-huit	DEEZ-weet
19	dix-neuf	DEEZ-nuhf

Putting Numbers Together— Mettre les chiffres ensemble

Numbers do a funny thing in languages— they start to repeat. Think of how you use the same "twenty" in "twenty-three" and "twenty-four." Or the same "thirty" in "thirty-six" and "thirty-seven." And how often do you use the same "seven" in "fifty-seven," "sixty-seven," "seventy-seven," and "eighty-seven"?

That means you just need to know a few numbers to know them all. In English, and in French, numbers between one and ten keep being used over and over. Take *vingt* (20) and add a *trois* (3) to make *vingt-trois* (23). If you start with *vingt* (20) and add *quatre* (4), you get *vingt-quatre* (24). And *sept* (7) appears in every seven number, such as *cinquante-sept* (57), *soixante-sept* (67), and even *sept mille* (7000).

Big Numbers—*Les gros chiffres*

French has a different way of representing numbers in the 70s, 80s and 90s. In French, 70 is 60 + 10, or *soixante-dix*. Eighty is four twenties, or *quatre-vingts*, and 90 is four twenties plus ten, as in *quatre-vingt-dix*!

Numeral	French	Sounds Like
20	*vingt*	van
21	*vingt-et-un*	van-TAY-uh
22	*vingt-deux*	van-DUH
30	*trente*	trant
40	*quarante*	CARE-rahnt
50	*cinquante*	SANK-ahnt
60	*soixante*	SWE-sahnt
70	*soixante-dix*	SWE-sahnt-dees
80	*quatre-vingts*	COT-truh-van
90	*quatre-vingt-dix*	COT-truh-VAN-dees
100	*cent*	sahn
1000	*mille*	meel
1.000.000	*million*	MEEL-yohn
1.000.000.000	*milliard*	MEEL-yard

Nouns—*Les noms*

Nouns are names of things. In English, you've learned that object names, like "pencil," are nouns. So are place names, like "Paris" or "San Francisco." And there are the "person" words, like "man" or "Theo," that are also nouns.

Since there are so many things in the world, we need a lot of noun words to keep track of the objects, places and people in our lives! Most of the words in any language are nouns. Here are some examples of nouns in both English and French:

You know how you write 33,515 with a comma between the 3 and the 5? Well, the French put a period there, so it's 33.515. Don't forget to swap your commas for periods when you write down big numbers!

English	French	English	French
desk	*bureau*	beach	*plage*
flower	*fleur*	star	*étoile*
bird	*oiseau*	woman	*femme*
cup	*tasse*	doctor	*docteur*
arena	*arène*	artist	*artiste*
restaurant	*restaurant*	Alexander	*Alexandre*

Singular and Plural—*Singulier et pluriel*

Just like in English, you add an "s" to the noun to say that there's more than one. One chair in French is a *chaise*, so two chairs are *chaises*. But words in French that end in a bunch of vowels get an "x" instead of an "s" to show they're plural. And words that end in "s" keep the "s," whether they're singular or plural.

Singular	Plural	Singular	Plural
bureau	*bureaux*	plage	*plages*
fleur	*fleurs*	étoile	*étoiles*
oiseau	*oiseaux*	femme	*femmes*
tasse	*tasses*	docteur	*docteurs*
arène	*arènes*	artiste	*artistes*
restaurant	*restaurants*		

Masculine or Feminine?—*Masculin ou féminin?*

In many ways, French nouns are just like English nouns—but in one way they're not. French nouns have "gender."

Gender means that there are masculine words and feminine words. For example, *fleur* is a feminine word, and *oiseau* is a masculine word. A few words, like *artiste*, are not really one or the other, so they get to be both!

To decide whether a noun is masculine word or a feminine word, all you have to do is learn whether it's preceded by a *un* (masculine) or a *une* (feminine). *Un/une* do the same job as "a" in English. Look at how it works:

English Noun	Masculine or Feminine	French Noun
a desk	M	*un bureau*
a flower	F	*une fleur*
a bird	M	*un oiseau*
a cup	F	*une tasse*
an arena	F	*une arène*
a restaurant	M	*un restaurant*

Learning "A"—*Apprendre "Un"*

French kids learn their nouns with an *un* or an *une* so that they remember whether the noun is a masculine or a feminine word. Why? Because it's hard to know which is which. There's no real reason why *étoile* ("star") is a feminine word and *vent* ("wind") is a masculine word, but it is: *une étoile, un vent*. It's difficult to explain. Better just learn your *un* and *une* from the start.

Both *un* and *une* become *des* in front of a plural word, no matter what the gender. So *un lit* becomes *des lits*, while *un vent* becomes *des vents*.

Verbs—*Les verbes*

Verbs perform action in every language—they are words that tell us what nouns do. "Eat," "read," and "sleep" are all verbs, just like "run" and "look." But French verbs do something that English verbs don't—or at least not in so much detail. They "conjugate." That means the end of the word changes depending on how it's used.

Les Fleurs

The Conjugation Map—*La carte de conjugaison*

Do you know what "conjugation" means? It means to change the form of the verb. In English, we conjugate a little bit. We say "she walks" but "we walk." The difference is the "s" for the singular, "she" who "walks," and no "s" for the plural "we" who "walk." French conjugation is fussier, but once you get the hang of it, it's fun to figure out which ending goes on the verb. There are a lot to choose from!

To match the noun to the verb, see if the noun is singular (I, you, he/she/it) or plural (we, you, they).

-ER Verb Map. *Manger* (to eat)

I eat	*je mange*
you eat	*tu manges*
he/she/it eats	*il/elle/il mange*
we eat	*nous mangeons*
you eat	*vous mangez*
they eat	*ils/elles/ils mangent*

-IR Verb Map. *Finir* (to finish)

I finish	*je finis*
you finish	*tu finis*
he/she/it finishes	*il/elle/il finit*
we finish	*nous finissons*
you finish	*vous finissez*
they finish	*ils/elles finissent*

-RE Verb Map. *Rendre* (to give back)

I give back	*je rends*
you give back	*tu rends*
he/she/it gives back	*il/elle/il rend*
we give back	*nous rendons*
you give back	*vous rendez*
they give back	*ils/elles rendent*

Translating Verbs—*Traduire les verbes*

Try and use the verb endings so you start to get used to them. Fill in the French equivalent of each verb phrase:

1. I eat _____   2. We give back _____

Now fill in the English for each French version:

3. *Vous mangez* _____   4. *Tu finis* _____

CHAPTER 2

Time and Dates—
L'heure et les dates

Telling Time—*Disons l'heure*

Knowing how to tell time is an important skill. How else do you get to school on time, share a dinner together, or know how long you can stay on the computer? Everyone on our planet agrees that sixty minutes equal an hour, and twenty-four hours equal a day. But the French tell time a little differently than Americans do.

Let's say a friend who lives in Detroit reminds you that a TV show you want to watch is on at 8 o'clock. You might have to ask, "Eight in the morning? Or eight in the evening?" In American English, "eight" can be by day or night, so we often add A.M. (from midnight to noon) and P.M. (from noon to midnight) to avoid confusion.

Counting the Hours—*Compter les heures*

The French use numbers to tell day from night without using A.M. and P.M. Eight in the morning is 8 (*huit*), but eight in the evening is 20 (*vingt*). This is because the French officially use a 24-hour clock. Instead of counting from 1 to 12 twice a day, they count all the way to 24. The first twelve hours are the same, but instead of starting over in the afternoon with 1 P.M., they keep on going with 13, 14, 15, and so on, until they get to 24. And instead of adding "A.M.." and "P.M.," or "o'clock," they add the French word for "hour," *heure*.

Since you already learned your numbers in the last chapter, you'll recognize them in the list of hours below.

English hour	Time in French	French hour
12:00 A.M.	*minuit*	00:00
1:00 A.M.	*une heure*	1:00
2:00 A.M.	*deux heures*	2:00
3:00 A.M.	*trois heures*	3:00
4:00 A.M.	*quatre heures*	4:00
5:00 A.M.	*cinq heures*	5:00

English hour	Time in French	French hour
6:00 A.M.	_six heures_	6:00
7:00 A.M.	_sept heures_	7:00
8:00 A.M.	_huit heures_	8:00
9:00 A.M.	_neuf heures_	9:00
10:00 A.M.	_dix heures_	10:00
11:00 A.M.	_onze heures_	11:00
12:00 P.M.	_midi_	12:00
1:00 P.M.	_treize heures_	13:00
2:00 P.M.	_quatorze heures_	14:00
3:00 P.M.	_quinze heures_	15:00
4:00 P.M.	_seize heures_	16:00
5:00 P.M.	_dix-sept heures_	17:00
6:00 P.M.	_dix-huit heures_	18:00
7:00 P.M.	_dix-neuf heures_	19:00
8:00 P.M.	_vingt heures_	20:00
9:00 P.M.	_vingt-et-une heures_	21:00
10:00 P.M.	_vingt-deux heures_	22:00
11:00 P.M.	_vingt-trois heures_	23:00

Asking about Time—_Demander l'heure_

Once you get the hang of the 24-hour clock, you have to practice using it. One way to do this is to ask questions about time.

Asking time questions in French is like asking about time in English. How long can I play? When do I have to be home? To answer time questions in English, you use "it is" followed by the number of the hour. "It is eight o'clock" or "it's 8:00 A.M." French kids do the same thing. They start with _il est_ ("it is") and end up with the numbers and hour, _Il est huit heures._ "It is 2 o'clock" is _Il est deux heures._

But things get a little trickier when you have to include the number of minutes. The French count the minutes in a way you've probably never seen before. They count backwards!

Counting Backwards—*Compter en arrière*

Here's how it works. In English, you always count toward the next hour. You say, it's "ten to three." But the French count backwards, so for them it's "three o'clock minus ten," or *trois heures moins dix*. And instead of saying "twenty to four," they say it's "four o'clock minus twenty," or *quatre heures moins vingt*.

But wait—there's more. You stop counting backwards at the halfway mark! So 11:30 A.M. is *onze heures trente*. And 1:15 P.M. is *treize heures quinze*, just like it is in English. You can also say it another way, too. In French, 11:30 P.M. is also *onze heures et demie* ("11 hours and a half") and 1:15 P.M. is also *treize heures et quart* ("13 hours and a quarter").

The following are a series of time responses to the question "What time is it?" (*Quelle heure est-il?*). Pay special attention to the words that name units of time. For example, "half an hour" is *une demi-heure*, and a "quarter of an hour" is *un quart d'heure*. Here we go!

English	French
What time is it?	*Quelle heure est-il?*
It's 10:00 A.M.	*Il est dix heures.*
It's 10:00 P.M.	*Il est vingt-deux heures.*
It's 1:30 A.M.	*Il est une heure trente.*
It's 1:30 P.M.	*Il est treize heures trente.*
It's 10:20 A.M.	*Il est dix heures vingt.*
It's 10:20 P.M.	*Il est vingt-deux heures vingt.*
It's 5 minutes to 4:00 A.M.	*Il est quatre heures moins cinq.*
It's 5 minutes to 4:00 P.M.	*Il est seize heures moins cinq.*
It's 12:30 P.M.	*Il est douze heures trente.*
It's 12:30 P.M.	*Il est midi et demie.*
It's 12:30 A.M.	*Il est minuit trente.*
It's 12:30 A.M.	*Il est minuit et demie.*
It's 15 minutes after 5:00 P.M.	*Il est dix-sept heures quinze.*
It's a quarter after 5:00 P.M.	*Il est dix-sept heures et quart.*
It's 15 minutes to 7:00 P.M.	*Il est dix-huit heures quarante-cinq.*
It's a quarter to 7:00 P.M.	*Il est dix-neuf heures moins le quart.*

Translating Time—*Traduire le temps*

See? It's not so hard! Now you try it out. Look at the time words that follow in English and write the French time words in the blanks. Use the number lists in the last chapter if you need clues:

1. 9:10 A.M. _____
2. 2:15 A.M. _____
3. 4:45 A.M. _____
4. 5:30 P.M. _____

5. 12:30 A.M. _____
6. 11:25 P.M. _____
7. 1:48 A.M. _____
8. 2:20 P.M. _____

Days, Months, and Years— *Les jours, les mois, et les années*

The French names of the days of the week are based on ancient Roman mythology. The French word for "moon" is *lune*, so Monday becomes *lundi*, or the moon's day. Tuesday is named after the god Mars, so Tuesday is *mardi*. Wednesday is dedicated to Mercury, so it's called *mercredi*. Thursday is Jupiter's day, so in French it's *jeudi*, while Friday is for Venus, so it's *vendredi*. Saturday is named after Saturn, so it's *samedi*. And Sunday is for the sun, which the Romans described as the day of the sun and which came to mean "day of the lord," or *dimanche*.

Instead of starting the week with Sunday, French kids name the days of the week starting with Monday. Check out the following list:

English	French	English	French
Monday	*lundi*	Friday	*vendredi*
Tuesday	*mardi*	Saturday	*samedi*
Wednesday	*mercredi*	Sunday	*dimanche*
Thursday	*jeudi*		

The months in French are just like the ones in English. The same letters are in both the English and French words. When words from different languages share the same group of letters, we usually say they share the same "root." Look at the following table and circle the shared root in both the English and French month words:

English	French
January	*janvier*
February	*février*
March	*mars*
April	*avril*
May	*mai*
June	*juin*

English	French
July	*juillet*
August	*août*
September	*septembre*
October	*octobre*
November	*novembre*
December	*décembre*

What Is Today's Date?— *Quelle est la date d'aujourd'hui?*

You know how to a write a date in English, don't you? You have to put the dates on your homework. And you need to know how to write dates for your history lessons. First you write the month, then the number of the day, and then the year. For example, you might write April 18, 2007.

The French use the same information we do in a date, but they put it in a different order. In French, the month goes in the middle, so it's *le 18 avril 2007*. They put the number of the day first, followed by the month, then the year. Even when they only use numbers for a date instead of words, they still write it so that the month is in the middle. April 18, 2007 is 4/18/07 in English, but 18/4/07 in French.

Compare the dates in the following list:

English	French
January 12, 1959	*le 12 janvier 1959*
1/15/59	15/1/59
March 21, 1992	*le 21 mars 1992*

3/21/92	21/3/92
May 2, 2005	*le 2 mai 2005*
5/2/2005	2/5/05
November 17, 2005	*17 novembre 2005*
11/17/05	17/11/05

The Year—*L'année*

Switching the place of the month and day is one thing; saying the year is another. You probably say the year the quick way, so "1996" is "19" and "96." Or for "1776," you probably say "17" and "76." The French do it the long way. For "1776," French kids say "one thousand seven hundred and seventy-six" or *mille sept cent soixante-seize*.

To say the year in French, you need to remember that it begins with the word for "thousand," *mille*. Then come the number of hundreds, like "nine hundred" or *neuf cent*, and then the number of years, like "ninety-six" or *quatre-vingt-seize*.

So "December 25, 2008" is *le 25 décembre 2008*, or *vingt-cinq décembre deux mille huit*, and "September 21, 1956" is *le 21 septembre 1956*, or *vingt-et-un septembre mille neuf cent cinquante-six*. It seems like a mouthful at first, but you'll quickly get the hang of it. French kids say *vingt-cinq décembre deux mille huit* all the time!

Look at the following dates and write the same dates the French way. The first one is done for you:

IMPORTANT TIPS
TRUCS IMPORTANTS

In English, the days of the week and the months of the year are capitalized. In French, they don't get capitals because they're not considered proper nouns.

1. *le dix juin mille huit cent quatre-vingt douze?* 10 juin 1892

2. *le quatre juillet mille sept cent treize?* _____

3. *le treize février mille cinq cent dix-sept?* _____

4. *le vingt-sept mai mille neuf cent soixante-et-un?*

   _____

MISTAKES TO AVOID
Fautes à éviter

Be careful when you write the dates using numbers. Put the numbers in the wrong order, and everyone gets confused. 2/12/08 looks like December 2, 2008 in French, not February 12, 2008. That's a big difference!

Parts of the Days and Year—
Les moments de la journée et de l'année

Now you know how to say the time, the day, the month, the year, and the date in French! Let's think of other ways you keep track of time.

You might look out the window at the light in the sky and decide it's time to get up. Or you feel a chill in the air and think it's going to snow. Sometimes you feel sleepy and you know it's time to go to bed. In fact, we can tell time not only by the clock, but also by what we notice and how we feel.

Morning and Night—*Le matin et le soir*

There are names for different parts of the day and night. Often, the names have something to do with the place of the sun in the sky. Every language has a word for "noon." In French, it's *midi*.

Here are some time words in French that you'll find useful for talking about time:

English	French
morning	*le matin/ la matinée (durée)*
noon	*midi*
afternoon	*l'après-midi*
evening	*le soir/ la soirée*
night	*la nuit*
midnight	*minuit*
day	*le jour*
today	*aujourd'hui*

English	French
yesterday	*hier*
tomorrow	*demain*
week	*la semaine*
month	*le mois*
year	*l'année*
summer	*l'été*
winter	*l'hiver*
spring	*le printemps*
fall	*l'automne*

Weather—*Le temps*

Like knowing what time it is, knowing the weather is also important. The weather tells us to put on a coat, open the umbrella, or get into a bathing suit. It makes you feel like playing in the leaves or going swimming.

The following list includes some ways to talk about the weather:

English	French	English	French
It's sunny outside.	*Il fait du soleil.*	It's windy.	*Il fait du vent.*
It's beautiful out.	*Il fait beau.*	It's bad weather.	*Il fait mauvais.*
It's hot.	*Il fait chaud.*	It's dark out.	*Il fait nuit.*
It's nice out.	*Il fait doux.*	It's daylight.	*Il fait jour.*
It's chilly out.	*Il fait frais.*	It's raining.	*Il pleut.*
It's cold out.	*Il fait froid.*	It's freezing.	*Il gèle.*
It's overcast.	*Il fait gris.*	It's snowing.	*Il neige.*

Practicing Weather Words— *Essaie les mots de temps*

Look at the following questions. Next to each question, write the answer in French. Since some of the questions have more than one answer, try and use as many of the French weather words as you can:

What's the weather like...

...when you go swimming? _____

...when you build a snowman? _____

...when you fly a kite? _____

...when you need to wear sunscreen? _____

...when you have to wear a sweater under your coat?

_____

...when you use an umbrella? _____

Holidays and Birthdays—*Fêtes et anniversaires*

One of our favorite ways of keeping time is with birthdays! You never want to miss yours, do you? No way—you want a cake and

presents. And don't forget about all the other fun holidays in the year!

Enjoying the Holidays—*Le plaisir des fêtes*

While French holiday traditions remain very strong, some American holidays are now celebrated in France. You'll recognize them on the following list. You'll also find some French holidays that are probably new to you, while other holidays, like the American holiday of Thanksgiving, won't be on the French list. But remember, a holiday is a holiday, no matter where it's celebrated!

Holiday Words—*Les mots des fêtes*

To say that the day is a holiday, French kids usually use "it is" and follow with the holiday name. "It's my birthday!" is *C'est mon anniversaire!* in French. Here they are:

English	French
It's my birthday.	*C'est mon anniversaire.*
It's New Year's Day.	*C'est le Nouvel An.*
It's Valentine's Day.	*C'est la Saint Valentin.*
It's Easter.	*C'est Pâques.*
It's Labor Day.	*C'est la Fête du Travail.*
It's Pentecost.	*C'est la Pentecôte.*
It's Music Day.	*C'est la Fête de la Musique.*
It's Independence Day.	*C'est la Fête Nationale.*
It's Halloween.	*C'est Halloween.*
It's All Saints Day.	*C'est la Toussaint.*
It's Christmas.	*C'est Noël.*

C'est mon anniversaire!

Time Questions—*Questions sur la date et le temps*

Asking questions about the time, the day, the date, and the weather in French is like asking questions in English. You use a question word like "what" or "when." You need a verb for "is" and then you need your time words, like "hour" or "year."

And you ask for the same information, "what time is it?" French kids ask that question just as much as you do, only they say it like this, *Quelle heure est-il?*

Question Words—*Les mots des questions*

To learn how to ask time questions in French, let's begin by looking at the question words you'll need:

English	French
when?	*quand?*
what?	*quel, quelle?*
how much?	*combien?*

Next, put the question words with your time word, such as *heure* and *jour*. Then add a couple of linking words, and you've got some great time questions. Here they are:

English	French
What time is it?	*Quelle heure est-il?*
At what time?	*A quelle heure?*
Do you have the time?	*Est-ce que tu as l'heure?*
What is the weather like?	*Quel temps fait-il?*
What day is it?	*Quel jour est-ce?*
When is vacation?	*Quand est-ce que ce sont les vacances?*
When is your anniversary?	*Quand est-ce que c'est ton anniversaire?*
What is the date today?	*Quelle est la date d'aujourd'hui?*
What is the date today?	*Nous sommes le combien?*
How many hours?	*Combien d'heures?*
How many days?	*Combien de jours?*
How many months?	*Combien de mois?*
How many years?	*Combien d'années?*
What holiday is it?	*Quelle fête est-ce?*

IMPORTANT TIPS
TRUCS IMPORTANTS

Don't forget to invert your subject and verb in a question, just like you do in English. You say, "what is it?" not "what it is?" The same thing in French. Say *Quelle heure est-il?* "What time is it?" not *Quelle heure il est?*, or "what time it is"!

FUN FACTS
Pour s'amuser

French kids sing "Happy Birthday" too—but they say *Bon anniversaire*. When the birthday boy or girl speaks French and English, he or she sings the song in both languages.

Joyeux Anniversaire

The twins are having a birthday party. Can you see the 8 differences?

Let them eat cake!

These words are attributed to Marie Antoinette, the Queen to Louis XVI, when the people of France had no bread to eat. But nobody really knows who said this. Marie was only 10 years old at the time the words were spoken.

CHAPTER 3

All About Me—
Tout sur moi

IMPORTANT TIPS

IMPORTANT TIPS
TRUCS IMPORTANTS

Contractions often happen in French when the verb begins with a vowel. *Je + ai = J'ai* ("I have") and *Je + aime = J'aime* ("I like").

les cheveux bouclés

Describing Myself—*Je me décris*

You know yourself really well, right? You know how you look, the kind of clothes you wear, and what you like to do with your time. All these things—and many others—make you who you are.

One way of describing yourself is with a "physical description." A physical description has mostly to do with how you look. It gives information about how old you are, how tall you are, how long your hair is, and a lot more.

When you give a physical description of yourself, you usually begin your sentences with "I." You say, "I am ten years old." French kids do they same thing, only instead of using "I," they use *Je*. In English, you follow the "I" with a verb, usually "I am" or "I have." The French equivalent is *Je suis* or *J'ai*. Finally, you finish the sentence off with a complement, like "I am ten years old." In French you'd say, *J'ai dix ans*.

But remember: In French, there are masculine words and feminine words. The feminine words usually get an extra "e," but every once in a while they get an extra letter or two. So the masculine word for "tall" in French is *grand*. The feminine word is *grande*, with an extra "e" on the end. The masculine word for "average" is *moyen*, but the feminine word is *moyenne*. You don't have to add extra letters all the time; some words, usually plural, can be used for both boys and girls.

Now let's look at basic questions and answers:

Your Name—*Ton nom*

English	French
What is your name?	*Comment tu t'appelles?*
My name is Alexander.	*Je m'appelle Alexandre.*
My name is Helen.	*Je m'appelle Hélène.*

Details About Me—*Les détails sur moi*

English	French
How old are you?	*Quel âge as-tu?*
I am seven years old.	*J'ai sept ans.*
I am nine years old.	*J'ai neuf ans.*
I am eleven years old.	*J'ai onze ans.*
I am fifteen years old.	*J'ai quinze ans.*

Hair Color—*La couleur de cheveux*

English	French
What color hair do you have?	*De quelle couleur sont tes cheveux?*
I have brown hair.	*J'ai les cheveux bruns.*
I have black hair.	*J'ai les cheveux noirs.*
I have light brown hair.	*J'ai les cheveux châtains.*
I have blond hair.	*J'ai les cheveux blonds.*
I have red hair.	*J'ai les cheveux roux.*

Hairstyle—*La coiffure*

English	French
What's your hair like?	*Comment sont tes cheveux?*
I have short hair.	*J'ai les cheveux courts.*
I have long hair.	*J'ai les cheveux longs.*
I have a crew cut.	*J'ai les cheveux en brosse.*
I have curly hair.	*J'ai les cheveux bouclés.*
I have wavy hair.	*J'ai les cheveux ondulés.*
I have straight hair.	*J'ai les cheveux raides.*

Eyes—*Les yeux*

English	French
What color are your eyes?	*De quelle couleur sont tes yeux?*
My eyes are brown.	*Mes yeux sont noirs.*
My eyes are blue.	*Mes yeux sont bleus.*
My eyes are green.	*Mes yeux sont verts.*
My eyes are hazel.	*Mes yeux sont noisette.*

Size—*La taille*

English	French
What size are you?	*Quelle est ta taille?*
How tall are you?	*Combien tu mesures?*
I'm tall.	*Je suis grand/grande.*
I'm average.	*Je suis de taille moyenne.*
I'm skinny.	*Je suis maigre.*
I'm thin.	*Je suis mince.*
I'm big.	*Je suis gros/grosse.*
I'm small.	*Je suis petit/petite.*

Right-handed? Left-handed?—*Droitier/Droitière? Gaucher/Gauchère?*

English	French
Are you right-handed?	*Es-tu droitier?*
Yes, I'm right-handed.	*Oui, je suis droitier.*
No, I'm left-handed.	*Non, je suis gauchère.*

IMPORTANT TIPS
TRUCS IMPORTANTS

The adjective often follows the noun in French. So instead of "red hair," you have "hair red," or *les cheveux roux*. And instead of "blue eyes," you have *les yeux bleus*.

TRY THIS
Essaie ceci

Imagine a Character—
Imaginer un personnage

Imagine you're someone else. Using your French vocabulary, create a new physical description. Give yourself different color hair, different hobbies, and a new name. Try to use as many French words as you can!

My Personality—*Mon caractère*

Do you like to laugh? Do you like to figure things out? Do you tend to look on the bright side of things? The answers to these questions describe your personality! How you think and feel about others gives information about who you are. Even your attitude toward food, art, and video games is part of your personality.

I am…—*Je suis…*

To describe your personality in English, you begin with "I am" and follow it by a descriptive word, like "friendly," to make the sentence, "I am friendly." In French, you do the same. You start with *Je suis* and add a descriptive word (also known as an adjective) to describe your personality. So "I am friendly" is *Je suis + sympa* or *je suis sympa*.

Here is a list of adjectives you will need. Both the masculine words and feminine words are listed.

English	French
I am	*Je suis*
happy	*heureux/heureuse*
content	*content/contente*
relaxed	*décontracté/décontractée*
curious	*curieux/curieuse*
funny	*drôle*
sensitive	*sensible*
friendly	*sympa*
athletic	*sportif/sportive*
shy	*timide*
artistic	*artiste*

English	French
full of energy	_en pleine forme_
healthy	_en bonne santé_
tired	_fatigué/ fatiguée_
nice	_gentil/gentille_
serious	_sérieux/sérieuse_
stubborn	_têtu/têtue_
cheerful	_gai/gaie_
active	_actif/active_
lazy	_paresseux/paresseuse_
generous	_généreux/généreuse_

I like…—_J'aime…_

Another way to describe your personality is by naming the things you like. In English, you say, "I like" followed by the complement, "I like playing the piano." In French, the word for "I" is one you already know, _Je_. The verb for "to like" is _aimer_. So French kids say, _J'aime_….

The complement that finishes off the sentence is usually a noun, a thing like "painting" (_la peinture_) or "swimming" (_la natation_). But sometimes the complement can begin with a verb, an action like "playing soccer" (_jouer au foot_). Then you make a sentence like _J'aime_ + _jouer au foot_, or _J'aime jouer au foot_.

The following are several ways you can complete the sentence, _J'aime_. Try to find the ones that apply to you:

English	French	English	French
I like	_J'aime_	tennis	_jouer au tennis_
dancing	_la danse_	soccer	_faire du foot_
singing	_le chant_	volleyball	_faire du volleyball_
playing outside	_jouer dehors_	playing music	_jouer de la musique_
games	_les jeux_	playing chess	_jouer aux échecs_
reading	_la lecture_	doing magic	_faire de la magie_
horseback riding	_faire du cheval_	taking photographs	_prendre des photos_
bike riding	_faire du vélo_	listening to music	_écouter de la musique_

I don't like...—*Je n'aime pas...*

Now think about the things you don't like to do, because that's part of your personality, too. Instead of adding "not" after the verb in English ("I do not like swimming"), in French you sandwich the verb between *ne* and *pas*. Be careful, though: If the verb begins with a vowel, you contract the *ne* to *n'*. So *J'aime la natation* ("I like swimming") becomes *Je n'aime pas la natation* ("I don't like swimming").

The Place Where I Live—*L'endroit où je vis*

Another way of describing yourself is by telling a close friend where you live. The best way of describing where you live is to begin by thinking about the big picture.

From Large to Small—*De grand à petit*

You live on the planet "Earth" (*la Terre*), right? Now let's think a little less big. In what "country" (*le pays*) do you live? Next, let's think a little smaller. What is the name of your "state" (*l'état*) or "region" (*la région*)? And now let's get more specific. Do you live in the "city" (*la ville*)? Or in the "country" (*la campagne*)? And do you live in a "house" (*une maison*) or in an "apartment" (*un appartement*)? Do you have your own "bedroom" (*chambre à coucher*), or do you share it?

Yes or No—*Oui ou non*

Going from big to little, or from more general to more specific, is often the way we communicate information about ourselves. Look at the following yes/no statements. Each question begins with "I live"—*Je*, followed by the verb *vis*—and by a complement that completes the sentence. So, if you're a French kid, you say, *Je vis en Europe* ("I live in Europe") or *Je vis en France* ("I live in France"). For each statement, answer "yes," *oui*, or "no," *non*. The questions get more and more specific as you go:

Je vis... en Europe (in Europe) Oui _____   Non _____

Le chant

Je vis… en Amérique du Nord (in North America) *Oui* ___ *Non* ___

Je vis… en Amérique du Sud (in South America) *Oui* ___ *Non* ___

Je vis… en Asie (in Asia) *Oui* ___ *Non* ___

Je vis… en France (in France) *Oui* ___ *Non* ___

Je vis… aux Etats-Unis (in the U.S.) *Oui* ___ *Non* ___

Je vis… dans une ville (in a city) *Oui* ___ *Non* ___

Je vis… en banlieue (in the suburbs) *Oui* ___ *Non* ___

Je vis… à la campagne (in the country) *Oui* ___ *Non* ___

Je vis… dans une maison (in a house) *Oui* ___ *Non* ___

Je vis… dans un appartement (in an apartment) *Oui* ___ *Non* ___

Je vis… dans une ferme (on a farm) *Oui* ___ *Non* ___

My Family—*Ma famille*

Another way to describe yourself is by your family. French kids have the same kind of words you do for their family members. Some of those words, like *papa*, will look very familiar! But in many French families, if one of your parents remarries, you may not always say, "This is my step-father." You simply refer to both your biological father and your second father as *père*.

"My" Is an Important Word—
"*Mon*" *est un mot important*
The following words are ones you need for describing your family. Notice how this time the nouns in French are preceded by *mon* or *ma* ("my"). The *mon* goes with masculine words and the *ma* goes with feminine words (except before a

papa   maman

frère   soeur

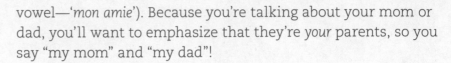

vowel—'*mon amie*'). Because you're talking about your mom or dad, you'll want to emphasize that they're *your* parents, so you say "my mom" and "my dad"!

English	French
my mother	*ma mère*
my mom	*ma maman*
my father	*mon père*
my dad	*mon papa*
my stepmother	*ma belle-mère*
my stepfather	*mon beau-père*
my sister	*ma soeur*
my brother	*mon frère*
my stepbrother	*mon demi-frère/mon frère*
my stepsister	*ma demi-soeur/ma soeur*
my grandfather	*mon grand- père*
my grandpa	*mon papi*
my grandma	*ma mamie*
my aunt	*ma tante*
my uncle	*mon oncle*
my cousin	*mon cousin/ma cousine*
my godfather	*mon parrain*
my godmother	*ma marraine*

I have...—*J'ai...*

To practice your family words—and your number words at the same time—fill in the following blanks. This time, instead of using *Je suis* ("I am") or *J'aime* ("I like"), you need to use *J'ai* ("I have"), the same way you do in English. If you say, "I have two sisters" in English, in French you say *J'ai* + *deux soeurs*, or *J'ai deux soeurs*. You add an "s" to the noun to make it plural. And if you're talking about girls—sisters, mothers, grandmothers, cousins—you have to add an "e" to the French word *un* ("one") to make it *une*. All the rest of the number words work for both boys and girls because they're plural:

J'ai _____ mère.

J'ai _____ père.

J'ai _____ soeur.

J'ai _____ frère.

J'ai _____ grand-mère.

J'ai _____ grand-père.

J'ai _____ cousins.

Pets—*Les animaux familiers*

If you have pets, you probably consider them part of your family, too. French kids are the same! They particularly like dogs in France. You see dogs all over Paris; they even go inside restaurants and stores. French kids also like cats, and sometimes have other kinds of pets, too.

Here's a list of pets in English and French. Some of the pet names are spelled differently for male pets and female pets. Others don't change at all.

English	French
dog	*mon chien/ma chienne/mes chiens*
cat	*mon chat/ma chatte/mes chats*
bird	*mon oiseau/mes oiseaux*
frog	*ma grenouille/mes grenouilles*
snake	*mon serpent/mes serpents*
hamster	*mon hamster/mes hamsters*
fish	*mon poisson/mes poissons*
insect	*mon insecte/mes insectes*

Excuse-Moi!

Fifi has knocked over the vase. Which one does it match when you put all the pieces back together?

French kids give their pets names, just like you do. To tell someone the name of your pet in French, you say *Mon chien s'appelle Whiska* ("My dog is named Whiska"). Or *Mon poisson s'appelle Blub* ("My fish is named Blub").

My School—*Mon école*

Describing your school is a fun thing to do. There are so many things to talk about! You can say the name of your school, the grade you're in, and the subjects you study. You can give the names of your teachers and what kind of activities you do. You can even describe the playground and what you had for lunch!

The Name of the School—*Le nom de l'école*

Start by describing the name of your school. "What is the name of your school?" becomes *Quel est le nom de ton école?*

You probably can already see how this question formula is put together. It begins with a question word, *Quel* ("what"). In French, "what is…" becomes *Quel est….?* Then we add the noun, just like we did in the other questions you saw. This time it's *le nom* ("the name"). Lastly we complete the sentence with *de ton école* ("of your school"). And voilà: *Quel est le nom de ton école?*

Now—how are you going to answer it? The easiest thing to do with questions is to use the same key words in your answer. So you begin with *Mon école* and follow it by your name verb *s'appelle*, and then you add the name. A French kid growing up in the *Luberon* area might say, *Mon école s'appelle Ecole René Char* ("My school is called the René Char School").

The Teacher's Name—*Le nom du professeur*

The next question is simple because you already know the question formula: *Quel est le nom de ton professeur?* ("What is the name of your teacher?") And you reply using the answer formula: *Mon professeur s'appelle…* ("My teacher is

named…"). But wait! Instead of "Mr.," "Mrs.," or "Miss," the French use *Monsieur*, *Madame* and *Mademoiselle*. Here's an easy chart so you can remember:

English	French
Mr.	*Monsieur*
Mrs.	*Madame*
Ms.	*Mademoiselle*
Miss	*Mademoiselle*

Your Grade—*Ta classe*

The next question—"What grade are you in?"—is a bit trickier in French. Not because the French language is difficult! *Quelle classe?* ("What class?") is easy because you already know the question word *quel/quelle* ("what") in French. And *classe* means "grade." The tricky part, *Dans quelle classe es-tu?* ("What class are you in?") has to do with names of the grades! French kids don't go to first grade, second grade, and all the rest. At primary school, the grades have long names that everyone abbreviates to save time. The French assign numbers to the grades in middle school and high school, except they count backwards! Here's how it works:

English	French
primary school	*école primaire*
kindergarten	*maternelle*
first grade	*CP1*
second grade	*CP2*
third grade	*CM1*
fourth grade	*CM2*
fifth grade	*CER*
middle school	*collège*
sixth grade	*sixième*

FUN FACTS
Pour s'amuser

In French, you can refer to someone you don't know as just *Monsieur* or *Madame* or even *Mademoiselle*. You say, *Bonjour, Madame* ("Hello, Ma'am."). In French, you don't have to follow *Madame* with her last name!

TRY THIS
Essaie ceci

Make a Schedule—
Fais un programme

Using the French 24-hour clock and your school schedule, translate your timetable into French. Write the hour and the subject you study, such as *11:00 - Biologie*, *13:00 - Musique*, and so on. That way, you can practice your French while keeping yourself organized, too.

seventh grade	*cinquième*
eighth grade	*quatrième*
freshman	*troisième*
sophomore	*seconde*
junior	*première*
senior	*terminale*
high school	*lycée*

I'm not—*Je ne suis pas*

To tell a French friend what class you're in, you use the familiar *Je suis*, add a linking word, and end with the name of the grade. *Je suis + en CP2,* or *Je suis en CP2* ("I am in second grade"). Since the French grade system is probably new to you, let's practice it a bit. Use the negative sandwich, *ne... pas*, like this: *Non, je ne suis pas à la maternelle* ("No, I am not in kindergarten"). Fill in the following sentences with the classes you're not in and finish with the one you are!

Non, _____.

Non, _____.

Non, _____.

Oui, _____.

My Subjects—*Mes matières*

Sometimes you want to tell your friends about the subjects (*matières*) you study. French kids study math, reading, and history, just like you do. Many of the subjects even share the same word roots. Here they are:

English	French
history	*l'histoire*
geography	*la géographie*
mathematics	*les mathématiques*
science	*les sciences*
social studies	*la sociologie*

biology	*la biologie*
spelling	*l'orthographe*
literature	*la littérature*
grammar	*la grammaire*
writing	*l'écriture*
French	*le français*
reading	*la lecture*
Spanish	*l'espagnol*
music	*la musique*
art	*l'art*
computer	*l'ordinateur*
physical education	*l'éducation physique*

You probably have subjects you like a lot, and maybe subjects you don't? On each line, write either *J'aime…* ("I like…") or *Je n'aime pas* ("I don't like…"), and fill out the complete sentence using the list of subjects:

J'aime… Je n'aime pas…

_____

_____

_____

_____

My Friends—*Mes camarades*

Your friends are an important part of your life. French kids have a lot of words for their friends. In English, you probably use different ones, too. You might have a "pal," and a "buddy."

Some friends you spend a lot of time with, and some you see only once in a while. Friends play different roles in our

les meilleurs amis

lives, and we refer to them in a number of ways. Here is a list of some ways you can refer to your friends in French:

English	French
my friend	*mon/ma camarade*
my friend	*mon ami/mon amie*
my pal	*mon copain/ma copine*
my pal	*mon pote*
my best friend	*mon meilleur ami/ma meilleure amie*
my best pal	*mon meilleur copain/ma meilleure copine*
my group of friends	*ma bande de copains*

CHAPTER 4

Social Life—
La vie sociale

Hi! What's Up?—*Salut! Ça va?*

Saying "hi" and starting conversations with friends is a handy thing in any language. So much can happen following a good "hi!" You can go play, go for an ice cream, talk about common interests, or just hang out. Your "hi" does more than offer a greeting; it can show someone that you're ready to talk or to have fun.

You probably already know a lot of different ways of saying "hi" in English. You might say "hey" to your close friends and "hello" to your teacher. And you probably follow up your "hi" with a "How are you?" or "What's up?" or even "How's it going?" You choose the kind of greeting depending on the person you're talking to.

For example, you probably speak more casually to your friends than you do with your school principal. You'd never say, "How's it going, buddy?" to your principal! You'd say, "How are you, Mr. Dumas?" In fact, you speak informally to people you know well and more formally to strangers.

French kids do the same thing, but they don't just change an informal "What's up, dude?" to a more serious "How do you do?" They change the "you"!

The Friendly You and the Formal You— *Le "tu" sympathique et le "vous" formel*

You need to know the two kinds of "you" in French because they are both used. There is the friendly "you," which is *tu* in French, and the formal "you," which is *vous*. Kids call each other by the friendly you, *tu*, all the time. But kids call older people, especially strangers, by the formal you, *vous*.

There's another important difference between the *tu* and the *vous*, and that has to do with the number of people the words refer to. In English, you can use "you" for one person or seven people. Not in French!

Salut!

The *tu* is singular. It always refers to one person your age or whom you know well. But the French *vous* is both singular and plural. The *vous* refers to one person whom you don't know well. And *vous* also refers to more than one person, whether you know them well or not.

Here is a table to help you remember:

Type of "You"	French Word
A friend	Tu
Someone about your age	Tu
Someone any age who you're close to	Tu
An adult you don't know well	Vous
An adult you're meeting for the first time	Vous
Any authority figure	Vous
More than one friend	Vous
More than one person you're close to	Vous
More than one adult	Vous

MISTAKES TO AVOID
Fautes à éviter

Try not to mix-up your *tu* and *vous* because it will confuse your French friends. If you call someone your age by *vous*, they may think you don't want to be friends. And if you call a friend's parent by *tu*, he or she may think you're impolite!

It's You!

Can you find the *vous* and *tu* hidden in this scene?

FUN FACTS
Pour s'amuser

The difference between *tu* and *vous* is so important in French that each word has developed its own verb. *Tutoyer* means to speak to someone using *tu*, and *vous-voyer* means to speak to someone using *vous*.

IMPORTANT TIPS
TRUCS IMPORTANTS

When you are unsure whether to use *tu* or *vous*, see which one your French friend is using. If he uses *tu*, you can, too!

Choosing Between You and You— *Choisir entre tu et vous*

Knowing when to switch from *tu* to *vous* is important in French. Because you don't switch between a friendly and formal "you" in English, you have to really learn to think about it when you speak French. You also have to learn to switch between a singular "you" and a plural "you."

Look at the following list and decide if the person or persons is/are a *tu* or a *vous*, and write the answer in the space provided:

1. Your best friend _____

2. Your teachers _____

3. Your mom _____

4. A bus driver _____

5. A kid your age you meet on the playground _____

6. Your friend's dad _____

7. Your doctor _____

8. Two police officers _____

Greeting Friends—*Saluer les amis*

When you switch the *tu* and *vous* in French, you have to change other things in the sentence, too. *Tu* goes with a singular verb, while *vous* goes with a plural verb. We discussed the different forms of the verb in Chapter 1 when you learned about conjugation. Well, now you get to see some conjugation in action.

Let's begin by looking at an important verb in French: *aller* ("to go"). The French version of "go" is just as versatile as the English one. Think of how you use different forms of the word "go." You've probably heard, "How's it going?", "Let's go!", "get going," "I'll go see," "keep going" and many others. The French verb *aller* does all the work of the English "to go," and more.

When you use *aller* in a sentence, you have to put the right form of the verb with the correct subject. Here's the conjugation map for the verb *aller*:

To go: Singular—*Aller: Singulier*

English	French
I go	*je vais*
you go	*tu vas*
he/she/it goes	*il/elle/il va*

To go: Plural—*Aller: Pluriel*

we go	*nous allons*
you go	*vous allez*
they go	*ils/elles vont*

Go, Go, Go!—*Allez, allez, allez!*

Now it's time to put the friendly you (*tu*) and the formal you (*vous*) with *aller* to say some French greetings. You can mix and match the questions and replies listed for *tu*, as well as for *vous*. But you can't mix the *tu* and the *vous*! If someone addresses you as *tu* in French, you usually call them *tu*, too! And the same thing for *vous*.

The Friendly You—*Le "tu" sympa*

English	French
Hi! How's it going?	*Salut! Ça va?*
Fine	*Ça va*
Good	*Ça va/ça va bien*
How are you doing?	*Comment vas-tu?*
Not bad	*Pas mal*

FUN FACTS
Pour s'amuser

When you ask someone how she's doing in English, you really don't expect to hear a lot of detail. Your friends usually answer with one word, like "fine" or "OK." Questions like "How are you doing?" aren't really designed to get information. They're more conversation-starters than real questions!

English	French
Not so good	*Pas très bien.*
How about you?	*Et toi?*
Is everything going OK?	*Tout va bien?*
Pretty good	*Pas mal du tout.*
Great	*Ça va très bien!*

The Formal You—*Le "vous" formel*

Hello Sir/Madame.	*Bonjour Monsieur/Madame.*
How are you?	*Comment allez-vous?*
Very well, thank you.	*Très bien, merci.*
Very well, thank you.	*Tout va très bien, merci.*
How are you?	*Est-ce que vous allez bien?*
Not so bad, thank you.	*Pas trop mal, merci.*
Not so bad at all, thank you.	*Pas mal du tout, merci.*
And you?	*Et vous-même?*
Everything is going well.	*Tout va bien, merci.*

"Hi" or "Hello"?—*Salut ou Bonjour?*

Greetings are easy to learn in any language because you have to greet people all the time! Anything you have to repeat often you usually learn quickly. Since you've been working so hard on *tu* and *vous* in this chapter, it's time to try them out. In each blank, fill in the right question or response:

Comment allez-vous? _____

_____ *Pas mal.*

Est-ce que vous allez bien? _____

Comment vas-tu? _____

Ça va? _____

_____ *Ça va très bien!*

Et vous-même? _____

Please and Thank You—*S'il te plaît et merci*

You know that part of being polite to others is saying "please" and "thank you." "Please" and "thank you" come in two versions in French, one for *tu* and one for *vous*. For your friends, you always use the friendly "you," and for adults and strangers you use the formal "you." Of course, if you're speaking to more than one person, you also have to use the *vous*.

Another "You"—*Encore un vous*

To say "please" in French, you need to conjugate a special verb, *plaire*. This verb does something very odd—it's "intransitive." When a French verb is intransitive, it insists on having a special pronoun!

The intransitive pronoun for *tu* is *te,* or *t'* in front of a vowel. So when you say "please" to your friend, you say *s'il te plaît*, which literally means, "if it's a pleasure to you." The intransitive form of *vous* is plain old *vous*, so to say "please" to an adult or more than one person, you say, *s'il vous plaît*. "Thank you" is *merci* for both, whether the "you" is friendly or formal, singular or plural.

> ## IMPORTANT TIPS
> ## TRUCS IMPORTANTS
>
> When you thank someone with *merci* in French, they often reply *je vous en prie*, which literally means "I pray you accept this service." Over time, *je vous en prie* came to mean "you're welcome." *De rien* ("it's nothing") is another polite way of replying to a thank you.

Mind Your Manners

Good manners are important everywhere, but be ready for new customs when you travel. Did you know it's considered polite to put your elbows on the table and keep your hands in sight when in France? Of course, it's always important to remember to say "please," and "thank you." Can you find your way through this *merci* maze?

Start

Finish

Here's a table to help you learn:

The Friendly You—*Le "tu" sympa*

English	French
Please	*S'il te plaît*
Thank you	*Merci*
Thank you very much	*Merci beaucoup*

The Formal You—*Le "vous" formel*

Please	*S'il vous plaît*
Thank you	*Merci*
I thank you	*Je vous remercie*
Thank you so much, Sir/Madam	*Merci beaucoup, monsieur/madame*

Inviting Friends Over—*Inviter des amis*

Having friends come over is a lot of fun! French kids spend time with each other after school and on weekends. They even have "sleep-overs" like you do. Now stop and think; what questions do you need to ask when you invite your friend over?

Use What You Know!— *Sers-toi de ce que tu connais!*

Remember how in Chapter 2, you learned about time and the days of the week? And in Chapter 3, you learned to explain in French where you live and what you like to do. Now you're going to use your French to invite friends over. That's the awesome thing about learning a new language—you can combine words you know in new ways to say new things.

To really make your invitations work, you have to add a couple of new verbs. Pay attention, because these are verbs you'll need! You'll use them as often in French as you do in

English. One is *pouvoir*, which means "can" in French. The other one is *vouloir*, which means "want" in French. They both follow the same conjugation map. Here it is:

Can: Singular—*Pouvoir: Singulier*

English	French
I can	*je peux*
You can	*tu peux*
He/she/it can	*il/elle/il peut*
Can: Plural—*Pouvoir: Pluriel*	
We can	*nous pouvons*
You can	*vous pouvez*
They can	*ils/elles peuvent*

The Conjugation Map—*La carte des conjugaisons*

You know how to read a map, right? You get from point A to point B by following the lines. And you try to find the best way of getting from point A to point B, too. The same thing is true of a conjugation map; instead of going from one place to another, you go from the subject to the verb. The subject and the verb have to "match"; not any old version of the verb will do!

You can't say "you goes" instead of "you go" in English, at least not without getting corrected! The same thing is true in French. You can't say *tu allez* when the correct form is *tu vas*.

To study how French subjects and verbs match up, look at the previous table, where *pouvoir*, ("can") is conjugated. *Vouloir*, the French verb for "want," follows the same conjugation map. All you have to do is change the "p" to a "v"! So *je peux* ("I can") is *je veux* ("I want"). And *nous pouvons* ("we can") is *nous voulons* ("we want").

TRY THIS
Essaie ceci

Sing Your Verbs—*Réciter les conjugaisons*

French kids learn to recite their verb conjugations in first grade. They do it so there's a kind of singsong rhythm to the recitation. You should try to recite, by heart, the conjugations you learn, too.

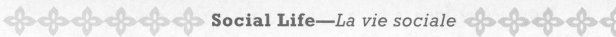

Asking Questions—*Poser des questions*

Questions are an important part of playing with friends. When you have some friends over, you'll ask them if they want to play basketball or watch a movie. Questions take different forms. Some use *quel/quelle*, *quand* and *combien*—the question words you learned in Chapter 2—and some are inverted! Sometimes they do both.

"Inversion" means "changing the order" of the words. You can think of it as "reversing" the order, because it's like going backwards. The difference between "Can you come over?" and "You can come over" is inversion.

"Can you" is inverted, because it's a question. The verb "can" goes in front of the subject "you." But "You can" isn't inverted, because "you" is in its normal place in most sentences. In "You can," the subject "you" precedes the verb "can."

French kids invert their questions just like you do. But instead of using "can," they use the right form of *pouvoir*, and instead of using "want," they use the right form of *vouloir*. Ready? Here are the questions you need to ask someone over:

English	French
Do you want to come to my house?	*Veux-tu venir chez moi?*
Can you come today?	*Peux-tu venir aujourd'hui?*
Can you come tomorrow?	*Peux-tu venir demain?*
Can you come after school?	*Peux-tu venir après l'école?*
Can you come for sleep-over?	*Peux-tu dormir chez moi?*
Can you ask your mom/dad?	*Peux-tu demander à ta mère/à ton père?*

Answer words—*Les mots pour répondre*

Questions always help you learn a language, because as soon as you learn the questions, you have most of, or even all, the words for the response. Sometimes you just need to add a *oui* ("yes") or a *non* ("no"), and start the sentence with *je* ("I"). And sometimes you have to get rid of the inversion.

IMPORTANT TIPS / TRUCS IMPORTANTS

French has more personal pronouns than we do in English. We have "I," "you," "he," "she," "it," "we," and "they." But French has *je, tu, il, elle, nous, vous, ils,* and *elles*. In English, you can't tell if "they" are boys or girls or both. But *elles*, the French pronoun for "they," tells us that the group is made up of all girls. *Ils* can be all boys, or a mix of girls and boys.

Peux-tu venir demain? ("Can you come tomorrow?") becomes *Je peux venir demain* ("I can come tomorrow"). Look at the answers to common invitation questions below:

English	French
Yes, I want to come to your house.	*Oui, je veux venir chez toi.*
I can come today.	*Je peux venir aujourd'hui.*
I can come tomorrow.	*Je peux venir demain.*
I can come after school.	*Je peux venir après l'école.*
I can come for a sleep-over.	*Je peux dormir chez toi.*
I'll ask my mom/dad.	*Je vais demander à ma mère/ à mon père.*

Now let's practice what we've learned. In the blanks, write the answer that goes with the question, or the question that goes with the answer:

1. *Peux-tu venir demain?* _____

2. _____ *Oui, je veux venir chez toi.*

3. _____ *Je vais demander à ma mère.*

4. *Peux-tu venir aujourd'hui?* _____

5. *Peux-tu dormir chez moi?* _____

6. _____ *Je peux venir après l'école.*

What Do You Want to Do?— *Qu'est-ce que tu veux faire?*

Once your friend comes over, you usually ask what he or she wants to do. Usually you ask if it's something you like doing yourself—building models, doing workbooks, putting a puzzle together. Remember in Chapter Three when we wrote down all the things you like to do? Now you're going to use

IMPORTANT TIPS! TRUCS IMPORTANTS

In French there are other common ways of asking questions. *Est-ce que* turns any statement into a question without inversion. *Tu peux venir chez moi* ("You can come to my house") becomes *Est-ce que tu peux venir chez moi?* ("Can you come to my house?"). Another way is *Qu'est- ce que,* which means "what." It gives us the popular question, *Qu'est-ce que c'est?* ("What is it?").

that same French vocabulary to ask your French friend what he or she would enjoy doing.

You set up the question using your *vouloir* ("to want") verb. Your conjugation map tells you that *tu* goes with *veux*. Now, add a little inversion, and you're on your way to constructing a good question!

English	French
Do you want to…	*Veux-tu…*
play outside?	*jouer dehors?*
go bike riding?	*faire du vélo?*
go to the park?	*aller au parc?*
watch a film?	*regarder un film?*
play chess?	*jouer aux échecs?*
listen to music?	*écouter de la musique?*
eat a snack?	*manger quelque chose?*

Now you're going to practice your questions by writing them as answers! Beside each of the following questions, write *oui* ("yes") or *non* ("no") and the answer, using the same words, but without inversion. Don't forget to change the pronoun!

For example, next to *Veux-tu jouer dehors?* ("Do you want to play outside?"), you write, *Oui, je veux jouer dehors* ("Yes, I want to play outside"). Or you can write, *non* and add the *ne… pas* sandwich we learned in Chapter 2. *Non, je ne veux pas jouer dehors* ("No, I don't want to play outside.") Here we go:

Veux-tu faire du vélo? _____

Veux-tu aller au parc? _____

Veux-tu regarder un film? _____

Veux-tu jouer aux échecs? _____

Veux-tu écouter de la musique? _____

Saying Goodbye—*Dire au revoir*

Saying "goodbye" to a friend is just as important as saying "hello." You use different kinds of goodbyes for the different people in your life. You probably say, "So long! See you tomorrow!" to your friends, while to an adult you may say, "Goodbye, Sir" or "Goodbye, Ma'am."

As you've probably guessed by now, there are "goodbyes" in French for the friendly "you," and for the formal "you." Here's a list of some you should know:

The Friendly You—*Le "tu" sympa*

English	French
Bye!	*Salut!*
See you later!	*A plus!*
See you soon!	*A bientôt!*
So long!	*Tchao!*
Let's go! Bye!	*Aller! Tchao!*

The Formal You   *Le "vous" formel*

English	French
Goodbye, Sir/Ma'am.	*Au revoir, Monsieur/Madame.*
Have a good day! Goodbye.	*Passez une bonne journée. Au revoir.*

CHAPTER 5

What Should We Do?—Qu'est-ce qu'on va faire?

Riding a Bike—*Faire du vélo*

Kids everywhere love getting on their bikes and heading off into the park, through the neighborhood, or down small country lanes. You take your bike, and off you go!

Part of the fun of riding a bike is finding your way, going over bumps and dodging potholes. You probably like to feel the wind while riding downhill, and everyone knows how good it feels when you finally reach the top of the hill.

When you're with a friend, you often say things to each other as you ride. You might say, "Here's the hill!" or "Slow down!" And because there's traffic out there, you need to learn to say, "Be careful!"

Riding Around—*Faire un tour à vélo*

Telling a French friend that there's a stop sign is easy! You have to put a noun and verb together, like you usually do. Some of those words you've learned in previous chapters. Some you're going to learn for the first time. Let's begin by looking at the key words you'll need:

FUN FACTS
Pour s'amuser

For over a hundred years, France has hosted a famous bike race called *Le Tour de France*. Cyclists from all over the world compete. Each race follows a different course. *Le Tour* includes high mountains, lots of curves, and thankfully, some flat stretches! It is considered the most difficult bike race in the world.

English	French
road	*la route*
street	*la rue*
corner	*le coin*
curve	*le virage*
hill	*la colline*
sidewalk	*le trottoir*
stop sign	*le stop*
driveway	*l'allée*
intersection	*le carrefour*
park	*le parc*
bike path	*la piste cyclable*
bike stand	*le parking à vélo*

Now if you're showing a friend around, you want to point out specific roads, hills and places. "Here's the park" in French is *Voici le parc*. And "there is" is *voilà* in French. So if you want to say, "There's the park," it's *Voilà le parc*.

Giving Directions—*Indiquer la direction*

When you're riding bikes with friends, you have to tell them to "slow down," "speed up" and "stop." And most important of all, sometimes you have to tell your friends to "Be careful!" Here's a list of some helpful words:

English	French
Slow down!	*Ralentis!*
Speed up!	*Plus vite!*
Careful!	*Attention!*
Traffic!	*Attention aux voitures!*
Stop!	*Arrête!*
Turn right!	*Tourne à droite!*
Turn left!	*Tourne à gauche!*
Brake!	*Mets le frein!*
Bump!	*Attention à la bosse!*
Keep going!	*Continue!*
You can do it!	*Courage!*
Great!	*Super!*
Time to rest!	*Repos!*

Playing Games—*Jouer à des jeux*

French kids like to play the same games you do. They like to chase each other, run, kick balls and hide. The girls chase the boys, and the boys chase the girls, just like they do at your school. Even the rules of the games are the same. When you're "it" in a game of tag, you have to run after everyone until someone else becomes "it"!

Here's a list of games you'll probably want to know:

IMPORTANT TIPS
TRUCS IMPORTANTS

One important and useful French word is *voilà!* You can use it to say "There it is!" or even "Look at this!" In fact, almost any time you need to draw attention to something, *voilà!* is a safe bet.

TRY THIS
Essaie ceci

Exclaiming in French— *Les exclamations à la française*

Try using French exclamations, like *Attention!* ("Be careful!") and *Super!* ("Great!") with your English friends. They might give you a funny look, but you'll be surprised at how many they instinctively understand!

English	French
hide-and-seek	*cache-cache*
tag	*jouer à chat*
climb tag	*le jeu de chat perché*
hopscotch	*la marelle*
jump rope	*la corde à sauter*
soccer	*le foot*
catch	*la balle au chasseur*
basketball	*le basket*
hot potato	*le furet*
Mother may I	*le merci grand-mère*
treasure hunt	*la chasse au trésor*

Do You Want to Play?—*Veux-tu jouer?*

French kids like some games more than others, just like you do. You may like to play tag some days, and other days you want to play basketball. Knowing how to say you want to play or not is important when it comes to having fun.

Negative Sentences—*Les phrases négatives*

Remember the verb *aimer* ("to like") from Chapter 3? And *vouloir* ("to want") from Chapter 4? You can use those verbs to say if you want to play a certain game. *J'aime jouer à cache-cache* ("I like to play hide-and-seek") or *Je veux jouer à cache-cache* ("I want to play hide-and-seek").

But what happens if you don't want to play a certain game? You can use your *ne... pas* sandwich to say you don't like something or don't want to play it. Just remember to sandwich the verb between the *ne* and the *pas*. *Je n'aime pas jouer à cache-cache* ("I don't like to play hide-and-seek"). *Je ne veux pas jouer à cache-cache* ("I don't want to play hide-and-seek").

Let's try it out. Answer each question below with *j'aime...* or *je veux....* But if you don't like to play the game,

use *je n'aime pas…* or *je ne veux pas….* Remember to use the words from the question to complete your answer:

Veux-tu jouer au foot? _____

Aimes-tu jouer à chat? _____

Veux-tu jouer à merci grand-mère? _____

Veux-tu faire de la corde à sauter? _____

Aimes-tu le basket? _____

Veux-tu jouer à la chasse au trésor? _____

Always and Never—*Toujours et jamais*

There are probably some games you always want to play, right? And chances are, there are some you never want to play, as well. Knowing how to say *toujours* ("always") and *jamais* ("never") is important in any language! In French, they're easy words to use.

To say you always like to play soccer, use the sentence you already know, only add the *toujours* just after the verb, like this: *j'aime toujours jouer au foot.* And if you want to say you never play a game, use your negative sandwich, only this time it's *ne… jamais.* So if you never like to play soccer, you say *je n'aime jamais jouer au foot.*

At the Park—*Au parc*

Parks are fun places, no matter where you are in the world. Lots of kids are usually there!

French parks come in all sizes, just like they do in other countries. In big French cities, like Marseilles, there are often big parks, with lots of things to do—sometimes even with *un manège* or an "amusement ride"! In small villages, like Goult, there are smaller parks, with basic "climbing

structures" (*des cages à écureuils*) and "slides" (*des toboggans*). But no matter what size the park, each one has special activities for kids.

The following is a list of things you can find in a park:

English	French
climbing structure	*la cage à écureuil*
sandbox	*le bac à sable*
tunnel	*le tunnel*
slide	*le toboggan*
swing	*la balançoire*
merry-go-round/carousel	*le tourniquet/le manège*
tennis court	*le tennis*
basketball court	*le terrain de basket*
soccer field	*le terrain de foot*
skateboard	*le skate*
roller skates	*les rollers*
scooter	*la trottinette*

MISTAKES TO AVOID
Fautes à éviter

There's a common confusion with the word for "soccer" in French: *le foot* (or *football*)! Many Americans think it refers to "football." It doesn't. The French don't play football!

"A" vs. "The"—*Un/une/des* vs. *Le/la/les*

You know the difference between "a skateboard" and "the skateboard in my closet" don't you? "A skateboard" is any old skateboard, anywhere. "The skateboard in my closet" is a specific skateboard. And that's the difference—"a" is any one, and "the" is a specific one.

French makes a similar distinction. *Un skate* is any old "skateboard," but *le skate dans le placard* is a specific "skateboard in the closet."

Often the words that use "the" have more information, so you know, without a doubt, that the object is special. But even when it's "the skateboard," or just "a skateboard," you know that one is more specific than the other.

You switch from "a" to "the" in English without thinking about it, since you've been doing it from the moment you began to speak in sentences. Babies can figure it out! They

know if they want "a cookie" or if they specifically want "the cookie" they see on the table.

French has a different "a" for nonspecific masculine words, feminine words and plural words—*un, une*, and *des* (some). And it has a different "the" for specific masculine words, feminine words and plural words—*le, la* and *les*.

Here's a table to help you understand how it works:

English	French
a ball	*un ballon*
a scooter	*une trottinette*
some skateboards	*des skates*
some scooters	*des trottinettes*
the ball	*le ballon*
the scooter	*la trottinette*
the skateboards	*les skates*
the scooters	*les trottinettes*

Review Time—*L'heure de la révision*

Let's try out the French version of "a" and "the." Look at the list, figure out the French words, and decide if the object is a specific one or not. If it is a specific object, use the *le/la/les* family of words. If it's not, use the *un/une/des* family of words. Then decide if it's singular or plural—if it's more than one, you have to use *les* or *des*. Then write out the complete answer in the blank:

1. a climbing structure _____

2. the merry-go-round _____

3. some swings _____

4. the basketball court _____

5. the roller skates _____

6. some slides _____

7. the soccer field _____

8. some tunnels _____

FUN FACTS
Pour s'amuser

France has some of the best museums in the world. In Paris, there are well over 80 museums to choose from, and little museums can be found in towns and villages throughout France. In Ménerbes, for example, there's *Le Musée du Tire-Bouchon* (in English, "cork-pullers"!). It's a museum where you can find a huge collection of corkscrews.

At the Museum—*Au musée*

Museums are fun places to go to when it's raining outside. Or when you want to exercise your brain more than your body. Museums are great places to "learn" (*apprendre*), to "study" (*étudier*), to "look" (*regarder*), and "have fun" (*s'amuser*).

There are many kinds of museums, but two main ones are art museums (*un musée d'art*) and science museums (*un musée des sciences*). Sometimes the art and science museums focus on a specific field, so you can have a museum of contemporary art (*un musée d'art contemporain*), a museum of modern art (*un musée d'art moderne*), a museum of decorative arts (*un musée des arts décoratifs*), a museum of photography (*un musée de la photographie*), a museum of Asian art (*un musée des arts asiatiques*), a museum of natural history (*un musée d'histoire naturelle*), a museum of technology (*un musée de technologie*), or a museum of archeology (*un musée d'archéologie*).

To Like and To Visit—*Aimer et visiter*

Let's work with the French verbs for "to like" (*aimer*) and "to visit" (*visiter*) to make sentences about whether you'd like to go to the museum or not. In the blanks, write either a positive sentence (*Oui, j'aime visiter le musée d'art contemporain*) or a negative sentence (*Non, je n'aime pas visiter le musée d'art contemporain*).

_____

_____

_____

_____

What *do you see?*—*Qu'est-ce que tu vois?*

At the museum, you get to see a lot of things. "To see" is *voir* in French. Here is the conjugation map for *voir*:

English	French
I see	*je vois*
you see	*tu vois*
he/she/it sees	*il/elle/il voit*
we see	*nous voyons*
you see	*vous voyez*
they see	*Ils/Elles voient*

And here's a list of some of the things you see in a museum:

English	French
an entry	*une entrée*
a ticket booth	*une billetterie*
a map	*une carte*
an exhibition	*une exposition*
a display case	*une vitrine*
a computer	*un ordinateur*
a guide	*un guide*
a sign	*un panneau*
an object	*un objet*
a painting	*une peinture*
a picture	*un tableau*
a sculpture	*une sculpture*

Replace "a" with "the"—
Remplacer "un" par "le"

Spend a whole day trying to replace each "a" in your spoken English with a "the." You'll be surprised at how much the meaning of what you say changes! And you'll learn just how important it is to use the right *un/une* or *le/la* in French.

Doing Sports—*Faire du sport*

French kids love to do sports as much as American kids, but some sports are more popular in France than they are in America. The French love "fencing" (*l'escrime*), which has been around since the Middle Ages, when knights in armor defended their castles. Another sport, archery (*le tir à l'arc*), has also been around for centuries. Of modern sports, the

FUN FACTS
Pour s'amuser

One of France's favorite sports is *pétanque or boules* ("balls"), which is played with heavy metal balls on a flat dirt surface. The idea is to aim your ball so that it rolls as close as possible to the marker. Many villages in France have several *boules* or *pétanque* teams .

French love "soccer" (*le foot*), but practically never play baseball or football. Oddly enough, the kids' word for "soccer" in French is more *le foot*. Here's a list of some of the other sports you know:

English	French
basketball	*le basket*
archery	*le tir à l'arc*
swimming	*la natation*
wrestling	*la lutte*
cycling	*les courses cyclistes*
fencing	*l'escrime*
horseback riding	*l'équitation*
golf	*le golf*

The Plural You—*Le "vous" du pluriel*

Remember how we learned to use the friendly you, *tu*, in the last chapter? Now it's time to learn to work with the plural "you," *vous*. Because sports are often played in teams. So you need to comfortable with the plural "you."

Here you will find sentences in English that you already know how to make in French. (If you can't remember a word, all you need to do is check back on the chapters you've done so far.) Now change each sentence from the *tu* form to the *vous* form. Use the plural verb forms: *vous aimez…* ("you like…") and *vous voulez…* ("you want…").

1. *Tu aimes faire de l'équitation.* _____.

2. *Tu veux faire du ski.* _____.

3. *Tu veux faire des courses de vélo.* _____.

4. *Tu aimes faire de l'escrime.* _____.

5. *Tu aimes faire du golf.* _____.

6. *Tu aimes faire du tir à l'arc.* _____.

Encouraging the Team—*Encourager son équipe*

Can you imagine going to a sporting event and not being able to cheer? Shouting to the team to run faster is part of the fun!

When you tell someone to do something, you give what's called a "command." That means there's no named subject. You just say "Go!" and it's clear who you're talking to. The verb is enough—you don't need the subject. But in French you can say "Go!" like *Allez!* or *Va!* You remember what the difference is, don't you?

Allez goes with *vous* and *va* goes with *tu*. That means you can tell if the subject is singular or plural, a friend or a stranger. In fact, the verb in French tells you a lot more than the verb in English.

Instead of having one way to give commands, you have three options in French. You can tell the friendly "you," *tu*, to score a point if you say *Marque un point!* But you can also tell the formal "you," *vous*, to score a point if you say, *Marquez un point!* And to the team you'd also say, *Marquez un point!*

Here are some commands you can give to the players in French:

English	French Tu	French Vous
Be careful!	*Fais attention!*	*Faites attention!*
Run faster!	*Cours plus vite!*	*Courez plus vite!*
Watch on your right/left!	*Regarde sur ta droite/gauche!*	*Regardez sur votre droite/gauche!*
Keep going!	*Continue!*	*Continuez!*
Stop!	*Arrête!*	*Arrêtez!*
Catch!	*Attrape!*	*Attrapez!*
Slow down!	*Ralentis!*	*Ralentissez!*
Throw!	*Lance!*	*Lancez!*
Hit!	*Frappe!*	*Frappez!*
Look!	*Regarde!*	*Regardez!*
Wait!	*Attends!*	*Attendez!*
Win!	*Gagne!*	*Gagnez!*

Now it's time to practice figuring out the subject from the verb. Look at the following verbs, and write in the line if the subject is *tu* or *vous*. It's easy!

1. *Lance!* _____
4. *Attrape!* _____
2. *Gagnez!* _____
5. *Frappez!* _____
3. *Attendez!* _____
6. *Arrête!* _____

At the Movies—*Au cinéma*

What kind of movies do you like? Funny ones? Adventures? Cartoons? French kids watch a lot of the same films you do. In fact, you can see your favorite films in French, and you can watch French films in English. The images stay the same, but the words change.

Sometimes the movies have the sound in one language, but the words are written in subtitles on the bottom of the screen in a different language. You can combine French and English in one film, and have a great time doing it, too. Next time you watch a DVD, set the language to French, and put the subtitles in English. You'll familiarize yourself with the French at the same time as you follow the story. In France a lot of things are dubbed, not subtitled.

Choosing a Film—*Choisir un film*

What kind of films do you like to see? Here is a list you'll probably recognize:

English	French
animated film	*un dessin animé*
western	*un western*
comedy	*une comédie*
adventure	*un film d'aventures*
science fiction	*un film de science-fiction*
detective film	*un policier*
spy film	*un film d'espionnage*
history	*un film historique*
drama	*un drame*
war	*un film de guerre*

> ## IMPORTANT TIPS
> ## *TRUCS IMPORTANTS*
>
> Remember that *ez*, *er*, *ais*, *ait*, and *é*, among others, are all pronounced like a long "a" in French. If you're ever in doubt about what ending to use on your verb, try the long "a" sound. It may not be right, but then again, it just may be!

Comparing Films—*Comparer les films*

Some kinds of films you like more than others. Maybe you might say, "I like adventure films more than comedies." When you say you like one thing more than another, you're making a comparison. Here's the formula for the positive comparison in English: I + like + film + more than + film.

The French comparison works the same way: *Je + aime + film + plus que + film*. So, if you want to say "I like adventure films more than comedies" in French, you say, *J'aime les films d'aventures plus que les comédies*. Since you're talking about kinds of films, you need to make plural nouns using *les*.

But you can also make negative comparisons. You can say, "I like adventure films less than comedies." In French, the negative comparison is formed with *moins*, like this: *Je + aime + film + moins que + film*. So if you say, *J'aime les films d'aventures moins que les comédies*, your friend knows you'd rather laugh than see some action.

The last kind of comparison is the "equal" comparison. In English, it looks like this: "I like adventure films as much as comedies." To make an equal comparison in French, you change the *plus/moins* to *autant*, so the formula looks like this:

Je + aime + film + autant que + film. The French sentence is: *J'aime les films d'aventures autant que les comédies.* Here's the formula:

English	French
I + like ____ more than ____.	*Je + aime + ____ + plus que + ____.*
I + like ____ less than ____.	*Je + aime + ____ + moins que + ____.*
I + like ____ as much as ____.	*Je + aime + ____ + autant que + ____.*

Since your comparison formulae are so useful, let's try them out. In the following lines, make positive, negative and equal comparisons in French:

_____

_____

_____

_____

Stripes and Balls

Everybody is doing well at *boules,* but some are doing better than others. Can you tell who has the highest and lowest score?

Here's a clue: Count the stripes on the players' shirts. The player with the most stripes has the highest score, and the player with the least has the lowest score.

CHAPTER 6

I'm Hungry!—
J'ai faim!

In the Kitchen—*Dans la cuisine*

The kitchen is a favorite part of any house. Because food is such an important part of French culture, the kitchen receives a lot of attention. The French are known for their food because it tastes really good! They pay attention to everything, including the best ingredients and the freshest fruits and vegetables. In general, they want quality more than convenience.

Tools and Appliances— *Outils et appareils ménagers*

You can probably name all the things in your kitchen with your eyes closed. You know that the ice cream is in the freezer, and the cookies are in the cabinet. You may even know how to put a pizza in the oven or steam vegetables. You're probably feeling a little hungry right now. Better learn your kitchen words, and fast!

TRY THIS
Essaie ceci

Labelling the Kitchen— *Mettre des étiquettes dans la cuisine*

Get some paper and some tape and label all the things in your kitchen. On the refrigerator write, *le frigo*, and on the oven, write, *le four*. Label as many things as you can. That way, every time you go into the kitchen, you'll practice your French!

English	French
cabinet	*le placard*
drawer	*le tiroir*
box	*la boîte*
container	*le récipient*
dish	*le plat*
bowl	*le bol*
basin	*la cuvette*
refrigerator	*le frigo*
freezer	*le congélateur*
oven	*le four*
pan	*la casserole*
microwave	*le micro-ondes*
table	*la table*
tray	*le plateau*
sink	*l'évier*
faucet	*le robinet*
dishwasher	*la machine à laver la vaisselle*

Savory Salad

Alain wants to make *une salade de fruits*. Which ingredients would he use?

la fraise

la poire

la cerise

les lardons

la viande

le jambon

la pomme

le poisson

la banane

le melon

There are lots of fruits and vegetables that sound very similar in French and English.

Can you tell what these are?
l'abricot, la carotte, le céleri, l'herbe, la lentille

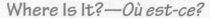
Where Is It?—*Où est-ce?*

Now that you have some kitchen words, you're ready to answer a common question: "where is it?" This question is frequently asked in a kitchen because someone is always looking for something—a bowl, a container, a dish. And it can be in so many places—in the fridge, in the sink, in the oven, and so on.

To ask "Where is it?" in French, you begin with the question word for "where," *où*. Then you add some words you've seen before, *il est* ("it is"). But because this is a question, you have to invert the subject and the verb like we did in other chapters. The question for "Where is it?" becomes *Où est-il?*

To answer this question, you use *Il est dans…* ("it is in…"). So if a French friend asks, *Où est-il?* you might answer, *Il est dans le frigo.*

In the blanks, write six responses to the question *Où est-il?* Use your new kitchen vocabulary for the answers.

_____

_____

_____

_____

_____

_____

Don't forget: You can take your "Where is it?" question, *Où est-il?*, and use it outside the kitchen, too!

Preparing Food—*Préparer un repas*

You probably know that cooking requires combining foods. So when you put a meat patty and a bun together, you get a

---

MISTAKES TO AVOID
Fautes à éviter

Conjugation is one of the hardest things in French. But you want to try to match your pronouns with your verbs whenever you can. If you incorrectly say *tu suis* instead of *tu es*, your French friends will understand you, but it might take a minute. They'll probably make a funny face, too!

hamburger. And when you cook some pasta and add some pesto sauce, you have pesto pasta. Or when you cut up some fruit and mix it up in a bowl, *voilà*, you have *une salade de fruits*, or "fruit salad."

But to make your favorite meals, you have to know what the foods are called in French. Here are some useful food words:

English	French	English	French
fruits	*les fruits*	ham	*le jambon*
apple	*la pomme*	meat	*la viande*
avocado	*l'avocat*	pork	*le porc*
banana	*la banane*	chicken	*le poulet*
cherry	*la cerise*	fish	*le poisson*
pear	*la poire*	turkey	*la dinde*
strawberry	*la fraise*	broccoli	*le broccoli*
melon	*le melon*	carrot	*la carotte*
raspberries	*les framboises*	potatoes	*la pomme de terre*
meat	*la viande*	green beans	*les haricots verts*
bacon	*les lardons*	spinach	*les épinards*
chicken	*le poulet*		

In the Fridge—*Dans le frigo*

It's fun to look in refrigerators, isn't it? You can tell a lot about someone by what they have in the fridge. Somebody with an empty refrigerator probably always eats out! And someone with a stocked refrigerator probably likes to cook for the family.

Here's a list of common foods your French friends will probably have in their refrigerator:

le poulet

FUN FACTS
Pour s'amuser

The French have a lot of cheese made from different kinds of milk. There's cheese made from cow's milk (*fromage de lait de vache*), cheese made from sheep's milk (*fromage de brebis*) and cheese made from goat's milk (*fromage de chèvre*). From the time French kids are babies, they eat cheese, even strong cheeses, like *Roquefort*.

English	French	English	French
milk	*le lait*	eggs	*les oeufs*
juice	*le jus*	olives	*les olives*
butter	*le beurre*	vegetables	*les légumes*
cheese	*le fromage*	fruits	*les fruits*
yogurt	*le yaourt*	cold cuts	*la charcuterie*

What Do You Like to Eat?— *Qu'est-ce que tu aimes manger?*

You probably like some foods a little bit, some foods a lot, and some foods not at all. Knowing how to say how much you like something is very useful, particularly if you'd like a second helping!

To tell a French friend how you feel about a food, you can say that you like it (*j'aime le fromage*), love it (*j'adore le fromage*), or hate it (*je déteste le fromage*). Using *j'aime…*, *j'adore…*, and *je déteste…*, write some sentences in French saying what foods you like, love, and hate:

_____

_____

_____

Drinks—*Les boissons*

Feeling thirsty after all this talk about food? Your French friends drink a lot of the same things you do, and some things that you probably don't.

French kids often sip wine (*le vin*) at formal meals—not because they want to feel funny, but because knowing about wine is, well, very French. And the best way to learn about wine is to taste it! So kids' taste buds are often trained from a very young age.

Kids' Favorites—
Les préférées des enfants

French kids also have a kind of soft drink, called *sirop*. It comes in all kinds of flavors—lemon, peach, even fig! You pour a little into a glass, add water, and *voilà*. When you add *sirop* to lemonade (*la citronnade*), you get a special treat, called a *diabolo*.

In the chart below, you'll find a list of French drinks:

English	French
water	*l'eau*
soft drink	*le soda*
syrup	*le sirop*
lemonade	*la citronnade*
kiddie cocktail	*le diabolo*
cola	*le coca*
wine	*le vin*
tea	*le thé*
coffee	*le café*

To Drink, To Eat—*Boire, Manger*

Now that you have words for things to drink, you need a verb to swallow them! Take a look at the conjugation map for *boire* ("to drink"):

English	French
to drink	*boire*
I drink	*je bois*
you drink	*tu bois*
he/she/it drinks	*il/elle/il boit*
we drink	*nous buvons*
you drink	*vous buvez*
they drink	*ils/elles boivent*

Spinning Spelling

What is this spinning fool telling us? Start reading the words from the center out and you will know what he likes to eat.

Since you've got a long list of things to drink—and the verb to do it with—you also need *manger*, the verb "to eat" to go with all your foods! Here it is:

English	French
to eat	*manger*
I eat	*je mange*
you eat	*tu manges*
he/she/it eats	*il/elle/il mange*
we eat	*nous mangeons*
you eat	*vous mangez*
they eat	*ils/elles mangent*

At the Table—*A table*

It's time to eat! In French, when you call everyone to the table, you say, *A table*, which literally means, "To the table!" And when everyone is assembled, you say *Bon appétit!*, which means "Have a good appetite!"

So let's get started. There's a tricky point though, and it's got a fancy name: *l'article partitif* ("the partitive article"). There are only four of them: *du*, *de la*, and *de l'* go with singular nouns and *des* goes with plural nouns. But although these words are small, they do an important job—they link the verbs *manger* ("to eat") and *boire* ("to drink") with the foods and drinks.

The Partitive Article—*L'article partitif*

You can't say, "I eat fruit" in French. You have to say, *Je mange des fruits*, because you need

76

 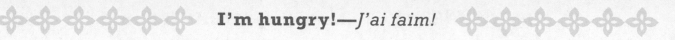

a linking word between the verb and the noun. It doesn't matter which form of *manger* or *boire* you use, whether it's the one that goes with "I," like *Je bois…*, or the one that goes with "they," like "*ils mangent….*" The important thing is that you've got a *du*, *de la*, and *de l'* between the verb and the noun, like this: *Je bois du lait* ("I drink milk") or *Ils mangent du poisson* ("They eat fish").

Here's a chart to help you out:

Je + *mange/bois* + *de la* + feminine noun.

Tu + *manges/bois* + *du* + masculine noun.

Elle + *mange/boit* + *de l'* + noun beginning with a vowel.

Vous + *mangez/buvez* + *des* + plural nouns.

What Are They Eating?—*Qu'est-ce qu'ils mangent?*

Often people ask what you ate for lunch or dinner. If they weren't at the meal, sometimes parents will even ask you what other people at your table ate. So you need to practice saying what everyone eats, and practice your *article partitif*, too.

Look at the following French sentences and translate them into English:

1. *Il mange du broccoli.* _____

2. *Elles boivent de l'eau.* _____

3. *Nous buvons du vin.* _____

4. *Je mange des carottes.* _____

5. *Tu bois du jus.* _____

6. *Il boit du sirop.* _____

7. *Vous mangez des cerises.* _____

8. *Ils mangent du poulet.* _____

I Don't Eat That!—*Je n'en mange pas*

Although it's a good idea to try and eat everything, often-times there's a food or two we can't eat often, or even at all. It might disagree with us, we might have health issues, or we might be too young to know that it's cool to eat lots of different things.

Saying you don't eat or drink something in French is easy. You use, appropriately enough, your *ne… pas* sandwich that we've used in other chapters. But watch out for *l'article partitif*! When the sentence is negative, all the *du, de la, de l'* and even the plural *des,* change to *de. Je mange du poulet* becomes *Je ne mange pas de poulet,* and *Il boit du jus* becomes *Il ne boit pas de jus.*

Change the following sentences from positive to negative by sandwiching the verb between *ne* and *pas,* and changing *l'article partitif* to *de:*

1. *Tu manges du yaourt.* _____
2. *Elle boit du coca.* _____
3. *Vous mangez du beurre.* _____
4. *Ils mangent du porc.* _____
5. *Nous mangeons des pommes.* _____
6. *Je bois de la citronnade.* _____
7. *Je mange de la dinde.* _____
8. *Tu manges des cerises.* _____

At the Restaurant—*Au restaurant*

French kids like to go to a restaurant with their friends and family. You get a chance to eat some wonderful French food in restaurants, foods that your parents may not have time to

IMPORTANT TIPS !
TRUCS IMPORTANTS

Knowing when to use *l'article partitif* can be challenging. If you can substitute "some" in the sentence, as in "I want some water, " then it's a fair bet you need *l'article partitif* in French. *Je veux de l'eau.*

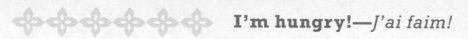
make at home. You may get to eat snails (*les escargots*) or a special kind of lettuce called *endive*, which is often served cooked! Even French kids who eat hamburgers also eat *lapin à la moutarde* ("rabbit with mustard sauce") because they've learned from a very young age to eat a variety of different foods.

The best part of learning about a new culture is trying its food. You don't want to go to France and eat hamburgers—that's something you can do in the US! In France, you want to train your *palais*, or your taste buds, to enjoy new sensations. You're probably in for a pleasant surprise!

On the Menu—*Au menu*

French kids know that French meals have three parts: *l'entrée* ("the appetizer"), *le plat* ("the main dish"), and *le dessert* ("the dessert"). A typical French meal has all three, so when you order in a restaurant, you have to give information about three dishes and what you want to drink!

Because the portions are smaller in France, you don't get nearly as much food on your plate as you often do in the US. In France, it's considered bad manners not to finish the food on your plate, so you tend to be served just the right amount. No leftovers!

Many restaurants serve traditional French foods. Here's what's on the menu:

MISTAKES TO AVOID
Fautes à éviter

When you're eating with your French friends, don't put a lot of food on your plate. The French serve a little, and then the kids ask for more if they're still hungry. If you leave food on your plate, it's considered bad manners!

English	French
first course	*entrée*
hard-boiled eggs with mayonnaise	*oeufs mayonnaise*
cold cut plate	*assiette de charcuterie*
vegetable soup	*soupe de légumes*
lettuce salad with bacon	*salade de laitue aux lardons*
oven-baked tomatoes with herbs and garlic	*tomates provençales*
main course	*plat principal*
steak and fries	*steak-frites*
omelet with mushrooms and ham	*omelette aux champignons et jambon*
lamp chops with mashed potatoes	*côtelette d'agneau à la purée*

Food Flags

In each group, which one of the food flags doesn't belong?

le lait

le sirop

le jus

tarte aux pommes

steak-frites

chocolat fondant

crème brûlée

les olives

le poulet

le jambon

le porc

la carotte

la dinde

How do they say "hello" in France? To find out just read the *béret*… but where do you start?

U O J
R N
B O

roast chicken with string beans	*poulet rôti aux haircots verts*
desserts	*desserts*
apple pie	*tarte aux pommes*
strawberry ice cream	*glace à la fraise*
chocolate cake	*gâteau au chocolat*
baked pudding	*crème brûlée / flan*

Ordering Food—*Commander un repas*

When you order food in a restaurant, you often use a special verb. It's a verb you know already, *vouloir* ("to want"), but this time we're going to use a polite form called the "conditional." *Je voudrais* is the equivalent of "I would like."

Like all verbs in French, the conditional has its own conjugation map. Here is the one for the conditional form of *vouloir*, "I would like":

English	French
to want	*vouloir*
I would like	*je voudrais*
you would like	*tu voudrais*
he/she/it would like	*il/elle/il voudrait*
we would like	*nous voudrions*
you would like	*vous voudriez*
they would like	*ils/elles voudraient*

The Polite Verb—*Le verbe poli*

Now we're going to order for everybody! Using your menu and the right form of *vouloir*, fill out the following sentences. Be sure and match the pronoun with the correct form of the verb! So if the sentence begins with *Je*, you follow it with *voudrais* and what you want to eat: *Je voudrais des escargots* ("I would like some snails").

1. *Tu...* _____

2. *Elle...* _____

3. *Vous...* _____

4. *Ils...* _____

5. *Nous...* _____

6. *Je...* _____

7. *Je...* _____

8. *Tu...* _____

Yum, Yum! That's Good!—*Miam, miam, c'est bon!*

It's very important to tell your French friends how much you enjoy eating their food! You need words like *C'est délicieux!* ("It's delicious!") and *Encore, s'il vous plaît* ("More, please"). Here are some words you'll find handy:

English	French
Enjoy your food!	*Bon appétit!*
I'm hungry!	*J'ai faim!*
It smells good!	*Ça sent bon!*
Time to eat!	*A table!*
It's good!	*C'est bon!*
It's very good!	*C'est très bon!*
It's excellent!	*C'est excellent!*
It's not bad!	*Ce n'est pas mal!*
I would like more, please.	*J'en voudrais encore, s'il te/vous plaît.*
More, please.	*Encore, s'il te/vous plaît.*
A little more.	*Encore un petit peu.*
That's enough, thank you.	*Ça suffit, merci.*
Is there any more?	*Y-en-a-t'il encore?*
There's no more left.	*Il n'y en a plus.*
I can't have any more, thanks.	*Je n'en veux plus, merci.*

CHAPTER 7

Going to Town—
Aller en ville

FUN FACTS
Pour s'amuser

France has a wonderful train system, called the TGV. The initials stand for *Train à Grande Vitesse* ("Very Fast Train"). It usually cruises at 186 miles per hour, but can attain speeds of over 200 mph! The TGV is recognized as one of the best train systems in the world.

Transportation—*Les transports*

There are many places to go to have fun, but first, you have to get there. French kids walk (*aller à pied*). They also take their bikes (*prendre leurs vélos*) or a skateboard (*prendre un skate*).

Maybe you've taken other forms of transportation, too. Look at the following list, and see how many you've used:

English	French
car	*la voiture*
bus	*le bus*
tour bus	*l'autocar*
subway	*le métro*
train	*le train*
ferry	*le ferry*
boat	*le bateau*
airplane	*l'avion*

How Will *We* Get There—*Comment s'y rendre?*

In order to use your transportation, you have to use a special verb—*prendre*. In fact, you don't "use" your transportation, as much as you "take" it. *Prendre* means "to take" or "to catch." You take a car (*Tu prends une voiture*), and even an airplane (*Tu prends l'avion*). So it's a good idea to study the conjugation map for *prendre*, just to make sure you get where you're going!

English	French
to take	*prendre*
I take	*je prends*
you take	*tu prends*
he/she/it takes	*il/elle/il prend*
we take	*nous prenons*
you take	*vous prenez*
they take	*ils/elles prennent*

Lucky you! You know one of the main French transportation verbs and several ways of getting where you're going. But wait—

what if you can't leave right away? What if "I take the train" or "I am taking the train" isn't exactly what you want to say?

Unfortunately, that's all you get with *je prends*. It's either "I take…" or "I am taking…." When a verb talks about "now" time, you say the verb is in the "present" tense. The same thing for all the other forms of *prendre* in the table above—they're "present tense." *Nous prenons* will always be happening now, as in "We take" or "We are taking." But what if you want to say something about the future? What if what you really need is "I'm going to take the train" or "We're going to take the train"?

The Near Future—*Le futur proche*

French has a very simple way of expressing the idea of "I am going to." You probably remember your French "to go" verb from Chapter 3, don't you? It's *aller*. In order to talk of an action in the near future, you need to conjugate *aller*. That means you need to match the forms of *aller* (*vais, vas, va, allons, allez, vont*) with the subject.

For the near future, you make a formula like this: subject + conjugated *aller* + *prendre* + type of transportation. So "I am going to take a boat" is *Je + vais + prendre + un bateau = Je vais prendre un bateau*. And "She is going to take the plane" is *Elle + va + prendre + l'avion = Elle va prendre l'avion*.

Look at the following present tense sentences and change them to *le futur proche*:

1. *Elles prennent un avion.* _____
2. *Il prend le bateau.* _____
3. *Nous prenons une voiture.* _____
4. *Je prends le bus.* _____
5. *Vous prenez un ferry.* _____
6. *Tu prends l'autocar.* _____

TRY THIS
Essaie ceci

Reading the Metro Map—
Lire la carte du métro

Paris has a wonderful *métro* ("subway") system. But it takes some time to get the hang of it. Ask your parents or your teacher to download a Paris metro map. Pick two metro stations at random, and try to figure out the best itinerary to get from one to the other! Try to find the direct route or change trains just once. A couple of itineraries require you to change trains twice. Can you find them?

IMPORTANT TIPS
TRUCS IMPORTANTS

While you "take" (*prendre*) a train, bus, plane, boat and car in French, you don't "take" your feet. If you're going to walk, you say, *Je vais à pied*, which literally means, "I go by foot."

There's a note left here, but it's in code. Can you figure out where Lucy is going?

Paris Puzzle

The first letter is in "love" but not "dove."

The second letter is the ninth letter of the alphabet.

The third letter is in "rubber" two times.

The fourth letter is in "Paris" and "France."

The fifth letter starts the alphabet.

The sixth letter has already been used.

The seventh letter is the letter a lot French people rrrroll.

The eighth letter sounds like what you see with.

The ninth letter shows up in "Eiffel Tower" three times.

Fun to do!

Once you figure this out, you can go, too! It's a great place to learn all about France.

Asking for Directions—*Demander son chemin*

Sometimes when you're going somewhere, you need a little help. Asking for directions is important in every language. How else will you find your way to the movie store for the first time? Or even find the bathroom the first time you visit a French friend's house?

Where—*Où*

You probably remember *Où* ("where") from previous chapters. And you know the difference between *est* and *sont* is the difference between "is" and "are." *Est* is singular, and *sont* is plural. *Voilà!* Two essential launch pads for direction questions:

English	French
Where is…	*Où est…*
Where are…	*Où sont…*

Destination Targets— *Destinations particulières*

There are so many places you can go, whether you're in a little town (*un village*) or a city (*une ville*). Let's list some of them:

English	French
The store/the stores	*le magasin/les magasins*
The bookstores	*la librairie/les librairies*
The library/the libraries	*la bibliothèque/les bibliothèques*
The movie store/the movie stores	*le magasin de film/les magasins de film*
The toy store/the toy stores	*le magasin de jouets/les magasins de jouets*
The department store/the department stores	*le grand magasin/les grands magasins*
The grocery store/the grocery stores	*l'épicerie/les épiceries*
The bakery/the bakeries	*la boulangerie/les boulangeries*
The restaurant/the restaurants	*le restaurant/les restaurants*
The bathroom	*les toilettes/la salle de bains*

MISTAKES TO AVOID
Fautes à éviter

Be careful not to mix up *la librairie* ("bookstore") and *la bibliothèque* ("library"). And note that "bathroom" is plural in French, *les toilettes*. If you say *la toilette*, you're talking about washing yourself! Another way to say "bathroom" is *la salle de bains*.

Spending Money—*Dépenser de l'argent*

Once you get to where you're going, you might have to spend some money. So you'd better be prepared!

French kids don't spend dollars. In fact, there are no dollars in France. And no cents! Instead you use the same kind of money that's used all over Europe: the Euro. In each Euro, there are a hundred *centimes*. The coins come in one, two, five, ten, twenty, and fifty *centimes*, and one and two Euros. *Une baguette* ("a loaf of bread") is about a Euro, a book is at least three Euros, and DVDs begin at seven Euros.

Here are some Euro words you might need:

English	French
money	*l'argent*
change	*la monnaie*
coin	*la pièce*
coins	*les pièces*
bill	*un billet*

Money Questions—*Questions d'argent*

When it comes to money, it's important to ask the right questions and understand the answers. You don't want to try to buy something you can't afford. Or misunderstand how much more you need to pay. Here are some questions and answers you'll probably hear:

English	French
How much?	*Combien?*
It's two euros and forty centimes.	*C'est deux Euros et quarante centimes.*
How much does it cost?	*Combien ça coûte?*
How much does the book cost?	*Combien coûte le livre?*
How much does the car cost?	*Combien coûte la voiture?*
It's five euros.	*C'est cinq Euros.*

It's twenty euros and eighty-five centimes.	*C'est vingt Euros et quatre-vingt-cinq centimes.*
Do you need more money?	*As-tu besoin de plus d'argent?*
More?	*Encore?*
It's expensive.	*C'est cher.*
It's too expensive!	*C'est trop cher!*
It's cheap!	*Ce n'est pas cher!/ C'est bon marché.*
Do you have change?	*Est-ce que tu as de la monnaie?*
I don't have change.	*Je n'ai pas de monnaie.*
Do you have enough?	*As-tu assez?*
I have enough.	*J'ai assez.*

Keeping Your Money Safe— *Garder son argent en securité*

It's not a good idea to keep money in your hand. You know why, don't you? Because you might lose it! You need to put (*mettre*) your money somewhere.

Mettre is an important verb. When we put food away, we use *mettre*. And when a French mom tells French kids to clean up their room and put things away, you can be certain she'll use *mettre*!

To Put—*Mettre*

Let's look at the conjugation map for *mettre*. It similar to the *prendre* map we used before:

English	French
to put	*mettre*
I put	*je mets*
you put	*tu mets*
he/she/it puts	*il/elle/il met*
we put	*nous mettons*
you put	*vous mettez*
they put	*ils/elles mettent*

TRY THIS
Essaie ceci

Collecting Coins— *Ramasser la monnaie*

Euro coins have the same value all over the world, but each country with Euro currency makes its own coins. France and its European neighbors—Austria, Belgium, Finland, Germany, Greece, Ireland, Italy, Luxembourg, The Netherlands, Portugal, Slovenia, and Spain—each put different pictures on the coins and bills. A fun thing to do is to try and collect a coin from each country.

Now we need the sentence formula, *Je* + conjugated *mettre* + *mon argent* + place = *Je* + *mets* + *mon argent* + *dans ma poche* = *Je mets mon argent dans ma poche* ("I put my money in my pocket"). Where else can you put it?

English	French
...in my pocket	...*dans ma poche*
...in my purse	...*dans mon sac*
...in my wallet	...*dans mon portefeuille*
...in my drawer	...*dans mon tiroir*
...in my backpack	...*dans mon sac-à-dos*
...in the bank	...*à la banque*
...in the safe	...*dans le coffre-fort*

The Recent Past—*Le passé récent*

Sometimes, saying "Right now, I am putting my money in my purse" *isn't* what you need. Neither is "Right now, I put my money in my purse." Sometimes you need, "A little while ago, I put my money in my purse." You want a way to say you did something recently in the past.

In French, it's easy to say that you did something a little while ago. You use a kind of verb form called *le passé récent* ("The Recent Past"). But to make *le passé recént*, you need another verb, *venir* ("to come"). Here's its conjugation map:

English	French
to come	*venir*
I come	*je viens*
you come	*tu viens*
he/she/it comes	*il/elle/il vient*
we come	*nous venons*
you come	*vous venez*
they come	*ils/elles viennent*

Show Me the Money

Tanya has ten *Euros* but she can't decide where to put them.

Can you help her by matching the name with the correct picture?

ma poche | mon sac | mon portefeuille | mon tiroir | mon sac-à-dos | la banque | le coffre-fort

FUN FACTS
Pour s'amuser

Conjugation maps show you how the verb is formed for six pronouns. The core of the verb usually stays the same, but the endings change. The three main verb groups— verbs ending in er, ir, and re— have characteristic endings. Every French kid has to memorize the differences between all the verb groups and all the irregular verbs, too.

To say an action took place in the recent past, you conjugate *venir*. That means you match the forms of *venir* (*viens, viens, vient, venons, venez, viennent*) with the subject.

Then you make a formula like this: subject + conjugated *venir* + *de* + *mettre* + Euros + place. So "I just put two Euros in my backpack" is *Je* + *viens* + *de* + *mettre* + *deux Euros* + *dans mon sac-à-dos* = *Je viens de mettre deux Euros dans mon sac-à-dos*. And "He just put a two-Euro coin in his wallet" is *Il* + *vient* + *de* + *mettre* + *une pièce de deux Euros* + *dans son portefeuille* = *Il vient de mettre une pièce de deux Euros dans son portefeuille* .

Since time is money, let's get going and try out *le passé récent*. Look at the following present tense sentences and change them to *le passé récent*:

1. *Elles mettent un billet dans un tiroir.* _____

2. *Il met son argent dans son sac-à-dos.* _____

3. *Nous mettons nos Euros dans un sac.* _____

4. *Je mets la monnaie dans le portefeuille.* _____

5. *Vous mettez vos Euros dans un coffre-fort.* _____

6. *Tu mets cinquante Euros et trente centimes à la banque.*

_____

Asking for Help—*Demander de l'aide*

Now that we have some money, it's time to spend a little. But what do you do when you're in a French store and you can't find what you need? You have to ask for help!

You learned in Chapter 4 that being polite is important in French culture. So you know you have to use the formal "you."

Begin with your polite opener, *Bonjour Monsieur/Madame/Mademoiselle*, followed by the "please" phrase, *S'il vous plaît*.

After you give the greeting, you can ask questions, "What color does it come in?" and "What size"? You don't need to learn *Combien* ("How much?"), because you already know it!

In What Color?—*Dans quelle couleur?*

Colors are a great thing to learn in any language, because otherwise the world is *noir et blanc* ("black and white")! Here they are:

English	French
black	*noir*
white	*blanc*
yellow	*jaune*
red	*rouge*
green	*vert*
blue	*bleu*
brown	*marron*
purple	*violet*
green	*vert*
blue	*bleu*

And here are some questions and answers that go with colors:

English	French
Do you have it in blue?	*Est-ce que vous l'avez en bleu?*
We have it in red.	*On l'a en rouge.*
Do you have it in yellow?	*L'avez-vous en jaune?*
It comes in green.	*Il existe en vert.*
Does it come in black?	*Existe-t-il en noir?*
Let me see.	*Je vais voir.*
I have it in white.	*Je l'ai en blanc.*
What's your favorite color?	*Quelle est ta couleur préférée?*
Pink is my favorite color.	*Le rose est ma couleur préférée.*

IMPORTANT TIPS
TRUCS IMPORTANTS

It's impossible to literally translate *le passé récent* into English! *Je viens de téléphoner* is literally "I come to telephone." But it means, "I just telephoned," or "a little while ago, I telephoned." When you can't exactly translate from one language into the other, you adapt the ideas as closely as you can.

FUN FACTS
Pour s'amuser

Although "red" is *rouge* in French, the colors are not exactly the same. They depend, to some extent, on the culture. Ask your French friends to show you "mauve" or "purple" or even "violet." It might not be exactly the color you have in mind!

What size clothes do you wear? What size drink do you want? And which size popcorn?

Knowing how to talk about size is very useful, especially if you want your clothes to fit! Size words are easy in French. And you've already seen some of them before in Chapter 2, when we learned words for physical description. There's *petit/petite* ("small"), *moyen/moyenne* ("medium") and *grand/grande* ("large").

Here are some other size words you'll probably find useful:

English	French
bigger	*plus grand*
bigger	*plus grande*
smaller	*plus petit*
smaller	*plus petite*
the same	*la/le même*
A little bigger	*un petit peu plus grand*
A little bigger	*un petit peu plus grande*
A little smaller	*un petit peu plus petit*
A little smaller	*un petit peu plus petite*

Now using the polite form of "I want it" (*Je voudrais*), get ready to make some size sentences. But be careful! Is your "it" masculine or feminine? Of course, the answer depends on what "it" refers to!

In these French sentences, the "it" is *le, la* or *les*. But it doesn't follow the verb. You put *le/la/les* in front of the verb. *Je la voudrais* ("I would like it" for a feminine word) and *Je le voudrais* ("I would like it" for a masculine word). And, of course, *Je les voudrais* for more than one thing.

To know if you want *le, la* or *les*, you have to know what the "it" refers to. If you're talking about a sweater, it's a masculine "it," because "sweater " is *le chandail* in French. And if "it" is a pair of shoes, it is plural, because "shoes" in French are *les chaussures*.

Choosing between *le, la* or *les* can get tricky when many words in the sentence have to show that they, too, refer to

a feminine, masculine, or a plural word. *Je le voudrais un petit peu plus grand* might refer to a sweater that you want a little bigger. And *Je la voudrais un petit peu plus grande* refers to a something that's a feminine word you want a little bigger.

Let's practice saying we want things bigger or smaller. Translate each of the following French sentences into English:

1. *Je le veux plus grand.*

_____

2. *Nous la voulons plus grande.*

_____

3. *Tu le veux plus petit.*

_____

4. *Il la veut plus petite.*

_____

5. *Elles veulent le même.*

_____

6. *Vous la voulez un petit peu plus grande.*

_____

7. *Ils le veulent un petit peu plus petit.*

_____

Activities—*Activités*

Sometimes you don't want to spend money on clothes or food. Sometimes you want to spend it on games and activities. In French, the verb for "to buy" is *acheter*. It follows the same conjugation map that *aimer* and other "er" verbs do. Here it is:

English	French
to buy	*acheter*
I buy	*j'achète*
you buy	*tu achètes*
he/she/it buys	*il/elle/il achète*
we buy	*nous achetons*
you buy	*vous achetez*
they buy	*ils/elles achètent*

Buying Tickets—*Acheter des tickets*

What can you buy tickets for? Here's a list to give you some ideas:

English	French
tickets for a soccer game	*des tickets pour le match*
tickets for the concert	*des tickets pour le concert*
tickets for the museum	*des tickets pour le musée*
tickets for the magic show	*des tickets pour le spectacle de magie*

Time for Tickets!—*Le temps des tickets*

It's time to practice your verb tenses. "Tense" is just another way of saying "time." You know three verb tenses now: the present (*le présent*), the near future (*le futur proche*), and the recent past (*le passé récent*). You can say that you're buying something, you are going to buy something, or you just bought something. Here's a chart to help you remember:

English	French
I'm buying two tickets to the movies.	*J'achète deux tickets de cinema.*
I am going to buy two tickets to the movies.	*Je vais acheter deux tickets de cinéma.*
I just bought two tickets to the movies.	*Je viens d'acheter deux tickets de cinéma.*

MISTAKES TO AVOID
Fautes à éviter

It's difficult for English speakers to put the "it" in front of the verb. When you say "I want it" in English, the word "it" follows the verb. But if you say *Je veux la* instead of *Je la veux*, you're telling your French friend that you want "there" instead of "it"!

IMPORTANT TIPS
TRUCS IMPORTANTS

There are two kinds of tickets in France. *Les billets* ("tickets") are for trains, planes and boats. But *les tickets* ("tickets") are for buses, movies, and the metro.

Let's Go Outdoors
—Allons dehors

In the Garden—*Dans le jardin*

French kids love the outdoors. Some houses have large yards, or *les jardins*, to play in. There are a lot of things to do and lots of things to look at, particularly in the spring (*le printemps*) and summer (*l'été*), when all the flowers are blooming. See how many of the following things are familiar:

English	French
lawn	*la pelouse*
tree	*l'arbre*
flower	*la fleur*
bud	*le bourgeon*
leaf	*la feuille*
sky	*le ciel*
cloud	*le nuage*
shade	*l'ombre*
shrub	*l'arbuste*
hedge	*la haie*
path	*le chemin*
umbrella	*le parasol*
fountain	*la fontaine*
patio	*la terrasse*

Here and There—*Ici et là*

Using *ici* ("here"), *là* ("there") and *là-bas* ("over there") is easy to do in French. And it's so necessary! How else are you going to find *le ballon* ("the ball")? Or each other?

To explain where something is, you need *être*, the "to be" verb, which we used in other chapters. Then you make a sentence formula like this: Subject + conjugated *être* + ici/là/là-bas + comma + place. So *Je* + *suis* + *ici* + , + *dans le jardin* is *Je suis ici, dans le jardin* ("I am here, in the garden"). Or *Le ballon* + *est* + *là-bas* + , + *derrière l'arbre* is *Le ballon est là-bas, derrière l'arbre* ("The ball is over there, behind the tree").

Here are some more words that you'll find useful:

English	French
on	*sur*
in front of	*devant*
behind	*derrière*
under	*sous*

Let's try your new words out. Translate the following French sentences:

1. *Elles sont là, devant les fleurs.* _____

2. *Nous sommes ici, sur la pelouse.* _____

3. *Tu es là, devant l'arbuste.* _____

4. *Ils sont là-bas, sous le parasol.* _____

5. *Je suis ici, sur le chemin.* _____

6. *Vous êtes là, derrière la haie.* _____

MISTAKES TO AVOID
Fautes à éviter

Try not to confuse *là* ("there") and *là-bas* ("over there"). *Là* is close, and *là-bas* is farther away. In fact, *là* is sometimes so close, that it seems more like "here" than "there!" The French use *là* when most English speakers would instinctively choose *ici*.

What Else Can You Find?— *Qu'est-ce que tu peux trouver d'autre?*

Yards are usually full of interesting things to look at and play with. You already know a lot of the words for things in the *jardin*. You know "bicycle" (*le vélo*), "skateboard" (*le skate*) and "ball" (*le ballon*). Let's see more here:

English	French
insect	*l'insecte*
hat	*le chapeau*
bat	*la batte*
cat	*le chat*
dog	*le chien*
bird	*l'oiseau*
frisbee	*le frisbee*
garden furniture	*les meubles de jardin*
hammock	*le hamac*
watering can	*l'arrosoir*
hose	*le tuyau*

You probably know what you're going to do with these things! You're going to put them in the garden. Try to make sentences like *Le chat est sous le hamac* ("The cat is under the hammock"). See if you can fill out the following sentences. And don't forget to make your subject match with your verb. If you can't remember which verb goes with which noun, turn back to Chapter 6 and look at the conjugation map for *être*:

_____ sont dans le ciel.

Les insectes _____.

_____ est devant la fontaine.

_____ sont sur la terrasse.

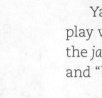

TRY THIS
Essaie ceci

Draw a Garden—
Dessine un jardin

Draw a picture of a garden. Choose as many of your French garden words as you can. Then label each thing with its French name. In the end, you'll have a pretty picture and practice your French, too!

Les oiseaux _____.

Le tuyau _____.

_____ est ici, dans le hamac.

Le frisbee _____.

Trees and Flowers—*Arbres et fleurs*

There are so many different kinds of flowers and trees! Some of them, like oak trees and daisies, you'll probably recognize right away. Others, like red poppies, you might not have seen before. In the spring, after a good rain, some fields in France are full of bright red poppies. They add lively color to the landscape. So do sunflowers and lavender.

In southern France, many beautiful trees and flowers grow in the Provence region. In fact, many visitors come to Provence just to see its colorful fields, gardens and parks. Here are some things that you might find growing there:

English	French
iris	l'iris
daisy	la marguerite
sunflower	le tournesol
tulip	la tulipe
dahlia	le dahlia
chrysanthemum	le chrysanthème
jasmin	le jasmin
cedar	le cèdre
oak	le chêne
pine	le pin
maple	l'érable
chestnut	le marronnier

Five French *Fleurs*

Can you find the five French flowers hidden in this *jardin*?

IMPORTANT TIPS
TRUCS IMPORTANTS

Remember that the noun is in charge of the sentence. Both the adjectives and verbs have to agree with it, in both number (singular and plural) and gender (masculine or feminine). Get in the habit of looking for words that match the noun. That way, when you're able to make long sentences, you won't make big mistakes!

Describe the plants—*Décris les plantes*

The world of plants, trees and flowers is lovely because it's so colorful. Do you remember your color words from Chapter 7? Let's try to "color-in" the plants in our sentences!

Compare these two sentences: *La marguerite est blanche* ("The daisy is white") and *Les marguerites sont blanches* ("The daisies are white"). You probably see the difference, don't you? One is singular and the other is plural.

As you know, the article, the noun, the verb and the adjective all match in French sentences. If the noun is singular, all the other words that go with it are singular. And if the noun is plural, all the other words that go with it are plural.

Here's a table to help you remember:

English	Gender	Number	French
The rose is red.	F	Singular	*La rose est rouge.*
The roses are red.	F	Plural	*Les roses sont rouges.*
The chrysanthemum is red.	M	Singular	*Le chrysanthème est rouge.*
The chrysanthemums are red.	M	Plural	*Les chrysanthèmes sont rouges.*

Did you notice that the color word, *rouge*, is the same for each flower, whether the name is masculine or feminine? Some adjectives go with both masculine and feminine words, and don't need extra letters. But when there's more than one flower, the color word usually gets an "s."

Time to "color-in" our flower and tree words! Using the first word—*le/la/les*—as your guide, fill out the following blank sentences. Follow this formula: *le/la/les* + plant name + conjugated *être* + plus color:

La _____.   *La* _____.

Les _____.   *Les* _____.

Le _____.   *Le* _____.

Matching Words—*Mots assortis*

Now that you're getting the hang of French sentences, let's add some other ways of describing flowers. Look at this chart:

English	Gender	Number	French
Beautiful	F	Singular	*belle*
Beautiful	M	Singular	*beau*
Beautiful	M	Singular	words beginning with a vowel or "h" *bel*
Beautiful	F	Plural	*belles*
Beautiful	M	Plural	*beaux*
Pretty	M	Singular	*joli*
Pretty	F	Singular	*jolie*
Pretty	M	Plural	*jolis*
Pretty	F	Plural	*jolies*

As you can see, there are five different ways to write "beautiful" in French: *belle, beau, bel, belles,* and *beaux*! This is because, in French, the adjective—the "descriptive" word—has to match the noun. So if the noun is a singular masculine word, so is the adjective. But if the noun is a plural feminine word, the adjective has to match, too. Here is a table showing "beautiful" in action:

English	Gender	Number	French
The rose is beautiful.	F	Singular	*La rose est belle.*
The roses are beautiful.	F	Plural	*Les roses sont belles.*
The chrysanthemum is beautiful.	M	Singular	*Le chrysanthème est beau.*
The chrysanthemums are beautiful.	M	Plural	*Les chrysanthèmes sont beaux.*

You see how it works, don't you? Every word in the sentence has to match the noun. Let's try it out. Write new sentences here using your garden words. Make the initial word *le/la/les*, the flower, and verb all fit with the adjectives. You can do it!

_____ *jolies.*

_____ *jolie.*

_____ *belles.*

_____ *jolis.*

_____ *beaux.*

_____ *joli.*

_____ *beau.*

_____ *belle.*

MISTAKES TO AVOID
Fautes à éviter

Don't confuse *bon* and *beau*. The pronunciation is similar, but the meaning is very different. The word *bon* means "good," as in, *Le hamburger est bon*. The word *beau* means "beautiful," as in *Les arbres sont beaux*.

At the Beach—*A la plage*

France has many beaches—some are in the South, along the Mediterranean Sea, and some are in the West, along the Atlantic Ocean. France also has a string of islands along both coasts, with beaches all the way around.

One thing that's very important at the beach is the temperature of the water! You probably say things like, "It's cold!" when you hesitate getting wet, or "It's not cold!" when you want your friends to jump in.

In French, you don't use "it" as often for water. Sometimes you use *l'eau*. You say, *L'eau est bonne!* ("The water is good") or *Elle est fraîche* ("The water is chilly"). And when you get out of the water and the wind blows, you say *J'ai froid!* ("I'm cold!").

Using "To Have"—*Utiliser "avoir"*

One of the most important verbs in French is *avoir*, which means "to have." Let's look at the conjugation map so you can get to know it a little better:

English	French
to have	*avoir*
I have	*j'ai*
you have	*tu as*
he/she/it has	*il/elle/il a*
we have	*nous avons*
you have	*vous avez*
they have	*ils/elles ont*

A la Plage

One of these kids went to the beach at the wrong time. Can you put these words where they belong?

froid | chaud | l'été | l'hiver

What season is it?

What season is it?

IMPORTANT TIPS

TRUCS IMPORTANTS

One of the most essential verbs to memorize in French is *avoir*. You'll need it to make verb tenses, just like you use "have" to do the same thing in English. For example, "I had seen" is *J'avais vu* in French. "Had" is used to make a verb tense in English the way that *avoir* is used to make a verb tense in French. The difference is that you'll use *avoir* a whole lot more than you use "have" because there are more French tenses!

To talk about how you feel temperature in French, you use *avoir* ("to have"), not *être* ("to be").

In English you say, "I am cold." In French, you say, *J'ai froid*, which happens to literally translate as "I have cold."

You use the same *avoir* map for getting hungry and thirsty. You say, *J'ai soif* for "I am thirsty" or *J'ai faim* for "I am hungry." At the end of a long, happy day at the beach, you may even say, *J'ai sommeil*—"I am tired."

The same thing goes for your friends, too. In French, you say, *Il a froid* ("He is cold") or *Elles ont faim* ("They are hungry"). But now here comes something odd: *faim, soif, froid,* and *chaud* don't change with the noun, whether it's singular, plural, a masculine word or a feminine word. But the verb still shows the difference between singular and plural!

Here's the map for *froid*:

English	Gender	Number	French
He is cold.	M	Singular	*Il a froid.*
She is cold.	F	Singular	*Elle a froid.*
They are cold.	M, or M and F	Plural	*Ils ont froid.*
They are cold.	F	Plural	*Elles ont froid.*

Now try to translate the following French sentences into English:

1. *J'ai soif.* _____

2. *Ils ont chaud.* _____

3. *Elles ont faim.* _____

4. *Elle a faim.* _____

5. *Elle a froid.* _____

6. *Nous avons chaud.* _____

7. *Vous avez froid.* _____

8. *J'ai sommeil.* _____

Playing at The Beach—*Jouer sur la plage*

What else do you need to say at the beach? You need to say you see something, *Je vois la mer* ("I see the sea"). And you need to say you want things, *Je veux le chapeau* ("I want the hat"). You may also want to say something is beautiful, *Le coquillage est beau* ("The seashell is beautiful"). Here are some words you might need:

English	French
beach	*la plage*
sea	*la mer*
water	*l'eau*
sand	*le sable*
sand castle	*le château de sable*
shore	*le rivage*
wave	*la vague*
temperature	*la température*
toy	*le jouet*
seashell	*le coquillage*
crab	*le crabe*
sea gull	*la mouette*
swimsuit	*le maillot de bain*
towel	*la serviette*
suntan lotion	*la crème solaire*
sun umbrella	*le parasol*

Now, using all your knowledge of French, fill in the blanks here to make complete French sentences:

Sur la plage, je vois _____.

Je suis sous _____.

Dans l'eau, je vois _____.

Il voit _____.

Les vagues sont _____.

Il fait _____.

Voici mon _____.

Le château de sable est _____.

Je veux _____.

Elles veulent _____.

At the River—*Au bord de la rivière*

Rivers are fun places to play in the summer. Some of the rivers in France come all the way from the Alps. The water is cold! And some of them, like the *Fontaine de Vaucluse* ("The Fountain of Vaucluse"), are springs that surge right out of the ground.

French Rivers—*Les fleuves français*

France has many rivers used for transporting people and goods, including *La Seine*, which flows into the English Channel; *La Loire*, which flows through the center of France, and *Le Rhône*, which empties into the Mediterranean near the city of Marseilles.

Since big cities usually grow up around rivers, it's not surprising that big French cities, like Paris and Avignon, are located on rivers.

Many of France's rivers transport people and goods. Boats called *péniches* carry *les voyageurs* ("travelers") and heavy things like *le sable* ("sand") and *les roches* ("rocks"). Some of your French friends may even live on *péniches* that have been converted into houseboats. In Paris, there are many restaurant boats and even a fire boat. The *Batobus* is a kind of river bus that takes people to where they need to go in Paris, and *le bateau-mouche* (literally "fly boat") is a kind of open-air tour boat on *La Seine*.

Smaller French rivers, like *La Sorgue* and *Le Calavon*, are perfect for fishing and boating, or just watching the wildlife. Can you think of the names of some rivers near where you live?

Many of France's rivers are protected by environmentalists so that the wildlife continues to thrive. There, you can usually see *canards* ("ducks") and *poissons* ("fish"). Here are some other things you can find on a quiet stretch of river:

English	French
a canoe	*un canoë*
pebbles	*des galets*
a fishing rod	*une canne à pêche*
a picnic	*un pique-nique*
a swan	*un cygne*
a dragonfly	*une libellule*
a mosquito	*un moustique*

Yard, Beach, or River?—*Jardin, plage ou rivière?*

In these blanks, write where you can find the thing or the action in the sentence. Use *à la plage*, *à la rivière* or *dans le jardin* in your answers. If more than one answer is right, then include both or even all three:

TRY THIS
Essaie ceci

Learn Your Animals—
Apprends tes animaux

Here is a game to play to learn your animals. Write all the animal names in French on index cards and put them in a stack. Then draw a picture of each animal on a different card and put the pictures in another stack. Shuffle the cards and try to match the word with the picture!

Voici le tournesol _____.

Je n'ai pas ma canne à pêche _____.

J'aime les vagues _____.

Il aime les châteaux de sable _____.

Le ciel est beau _____.

Je vois un chêne _____.

Je veux de la crème solaire _____.

J'ai des coquillages _____.

Nous n'aimons pas les moustiques _____.

Les cygnes sont beaux _____.

At the Zoo—*Au zoo*

There are so many interesting animals at the zoo! The zoos in France are a lot like the ones you've been to, except they're a little smaller. A little zoo in France even has a special name. It's called *une ménagerie,* and it is usually attached to a circus.

But the animals you see in French zoos are the same ones you go to see in other countries. Here's a list of some familiar ones:

English	French
a zebra	*un zèbre*
a giraffe	*une girafe*
an elephant	*un éléphant*
an ostrich	*une autruche*
a tiger	*un tigre*
a bear	*un ours*
a snake	*un serpent*
a crocodile	*un crocodile*

The Past Tense—*Les temps du passé*

You remember how in previous chapter, we learned to use *le futur proche* ("the near future") and *le passé recent* ("the recent past")?

To say "I see the lion" in French, you use the conjugation map for the present tense and write, *Je vois le lion.* If you want to say, "I just saw a lion" (a little while ago), you use *le passé récent* and write, *Je viens de voir un lion.* And if you're going to see a lion, you use *le futur proche* and say or write, *Je vais voir le lion.*

But what if you saw the lion? Not "today" (*aujourd'hui*), but "yesterday" (*hier*)? You need to say, *J'ai vu le lion.*

For an action in the past, you often use *le passé composé.* If you saw something yesterday at the zoo, you use the formula like this: subject + conjugated *avoir* + past verb (past participle) + name of animal. So, to say, "She saw a lion" you use *elle + a + vu + un lion = Elle a vu un lion.* Or, if you want to remind a group of people that they saw a lion, you use *Vous + avez + vu + un lion = Vous avez vu un lion.*

IMPORTANT TIPS
TRUCS IMPORTANTS

French has more ways to speak about the past than English does. You have "I walked," "I was walking," "I had walked," and "I had been walking." That means English has four tenses, or four ways, to speak of an action in the past. French has six! All the more reason to learn your French verbs slowly, one at a time.

You Saw It Yesterday!— *Vous l'avez vu hier!*

Change the following present tense sentences to past tense using *le passé composé* formula. If you can't remember your conjugation map for *avoir*, look back through this chapter. Write the entire past tense sentence in the blank:

1. *Je vois un zèbre.*

   _____.

2. *Nous voyons une girafe.*

   _____.

3. *Elles voient un éléphant.*

   _____.

4. *Il voit une autruche.*

   _____.

Sketch at the Zoo

The Etch-a-Sketch® was invented by Arthur Granjean from France in 1960. Can you finish sketching these animals?

5. *Tu vois un tigre.*

_____.

6. *Il voit un ours.*

_____.

7. *Ils voient un serpent.*

_____.

8. *Nous voyons un crocodile.*

_____.

On the Farm—*A la ferme*

In the French countryside, you can see a lot of animals on farms. Animals like sheep and cows are raised for both meat and cheese. Pigs are raised for pork, but also to do some important work—finding very special mushrooms, called *truffes*, that pigs are able to smell more easily than dogs can. And many French farms have horses and chickens, too.

Here's a list of common farm animals:

English	French
a horse	*un cheval/des chevaux*
a goat	*une chèvre/des chèvres*
a sheep	*un mouton/des moutons*
a pig	*un cochon/des cochons*
a goose	*un oie/des oies*
a chicken	*un poulet/des poulets*
a rooster	*un coq/des coqs*

Let's Feed the Animals— *Nous allons nourir les animaux*

Farm animals eat simple things. They eat *du blé* ("wheat"), *du foin* ("hay"), *des grains* ("grains")

and *de l'herbe* ("grass"). You remember the verb "to eat," *manger*, from previous chapters, don't you? So, if you want to say that "the horse eats hay" in French, you write, *Le cheval mange du foin*.

Let's see if you can fill out the blanks in the following French sentences. If you need help remembering the conjugation map for *manger* or *boire*, check them out in Chapter 6.

Les poulets mangent _____.

Le cochon _____ *du blé.*

_____ *ne mange pas de grains.*

_____ *mange* _____.

_____ *ne boivent pas* _____.

Le coq boit _____.

Put It in the Past—*Mets-le au passé*

You know how to say you saw something in the past, right? You saw above that you use *le passé composé*. You use *Je* + conjugated *avoir* + *vu*.

Now guess how you say that an animal *ate* something yesterday? You're right—you use *le passé composé*. Only this time, instead of using the past participle *vu*, you use the past participle *mangé*.

So to say, "the cow ate the grass," you say *La vache a mangé l'herbe*. Or if you mean "the horses ate the grass" in French, you write, *Les chevaux ont mangé l'herbe*.

Since you're doing so well, let's try to put your "to drink" verb, *boire*, in the past, too. So this time, instead of using *vu* or *mangé*, you put *bu* in the *passé composé* formula. "The sheep drank water," is *Les moutons ont bu de l'eau*. And "the rooster drank water" is *Le coq a bu de l'eau*.

FUN FACTS
Pour s'amuser

Animals make different sounds in different languages. In French, a pig says *gronk-gronk*, a duck *coin-coin*, a rooster *cocorico*, a cow *meuh*, a sheep *bêê-bêê*, a cat *miaou*, and a dog *woua-woua*.

Time to practice the *passé composé* using your new verbs. Write six sentences here with vocabulary words from this chapter and the *passé composé* forms of *mangé, bu,* and *vu:*

_____

_____

_____

_____

_____

_____

_____

CHAPTER 9

Getting Along—
Bien s'entendre

Best Friends—*Les meilleurs amis*

French kids like to have special friends, just like you do! But instead of having "a best friend" or "my best friends," there are more possibilities to choose from! Here are some of the possibilities for the word *ami* ("friend") in French:

English	Gender	Number	French
Friend	M	Singular	*ami*
Friend	F	Singular	*amie*
Friends	M	Plural Boys, or Boys and Girls	*amis*
Friends	F	Plural	*amies*

Matching the Adjectives— *Accorder les adjectifs*

To explain who your best friends are, you need to add the adjective "best" to your "friend" word, *ami*. Here's the map for the word *meilleur* in French:

English	Gender	Number	French
My best	M	Singular	*mon meilleur*
My best	F	Singular	*ma meilleure*
My best	M	Plural M, or M and F	*mes meilleurs*
My best	F	Plural	*mes meilleures*

To make a sentence like, "Andrew, Noah, and Theo are my best friends," you need the following formula: Names + are + my best friends. In French, the formula is: *Noms + sont + mes meilleurs amis*. "Andrew, Noah, and Theo are my best friends" becomes *Andrew, Noah et Theo sont mes meilleurs amis* in French. Notice that the name, the verb, the article, the adjective and the noun all match!

Tous Les Amis

All these kids are different—and that's a good thing. But one of them likes to be the most different. Can you find who has all these characteristics?

a *béret*, an earring on the right ear, a big smile, no glasses, a striped shirt

My Lovely Béret

Here's a fun activity: Write your own song about a *béret*. The *béret* is worn all over the world, but is known as a French symbol. Here are a few rhyming words to get you started: Monday, today, away. Have fun!

MISTAKES TO AVOID
Fautes à éviter

The more words in a French sentence, the more you have to pay attention. If you start off a sentence with a feminine word and end the same sentence with masculine words, you will probably confuse your French friends. Don't forget to make all the words in your sentence match!

The same thing happens in this sentence: "Solène is my best friend." You need the name + verb + article + adjective + noun to match. Here is the sentence in French: *Solène est ma meilleure amie.*

Let's see how you do. Fill out the following sentences with the names your best friends, the real ones and the pretend ones!

_____ est mon meilleur ami.

_____ sont mes meilleures amies.

_____ est ma meilleure amie.

_____ sont mes meilleurs amis.

His and Her Friends—*Leurs amis*

Sometimes you want to talk about your friends' friends, too. There is an easy way to do this.

Remember the words for "my," the *ma/mon/mes* articles you learned in Chapter 3? To say "his" and "her," you follow the same pattern as *ma/mon/mes*. They're a cinch to learn. The trick is to remember that the French word you use for "his" or "her" goes with the best friend. Look at the map below:

English	Gender	Number	French
His/her best friend	M	Singular	*son meilleur ami*
His/her best friend	F	Singular	*sa meilleure amie*
His/her best friend	M	Plural M, or M and F	*ses meilleurs amis*
His/her best friend	F	Plural	*ses meilleures amies*

To say that "Anouk is her best friend" in French, you say, *Anouk est sa meilleure amie.* And to say that "Arthur, Axil, Leonard and Louis are his best friends," you say, *Arthur, Axil,*

Leonard et Louis sont ses meilleurs amis. But you'd also use *ses meilleurs amis* if the friends in question are Alyna, Leo, Eliza, and Sophie! Let's see if you got the hang of it. Fill out the following sentences. Remember to choose girl and boy names as needed:

> _____ est son meilleur ami.
>
> _____ sont ses meilleures amies.
>
> _____ est sa meilleure amie.
>
> _____ sont ses meilleurs amis.

> **IMPORTANT TIPS!**
> **TRUCS IMPORTANTS**
>
> The written French language is more complex than spoken French. If you say *ami* and *amie*, they sound the same. So do *amis* and *amies*. But the feminine and masculine words make a big difference in the rest of the sentence!

Now let's review of all the things you've learned so far in this chapter. Translate the following English sentences into French:

1. Theo is his best friend. _____

2. Noah is his best friend. _____

3. Solène is his best friend. _____

4. Ebba, Gwen, Lisa and Nikki are her best friends. _____

5. Laurent and Philippe are her best friends. _____

6. Jeanette, Philippe and Sally are her best friends. _____

7. Jody and Kiko are his best friends. _____

8. Jeanette is his best friend. _____

Expressing Feelings—*Exprimer ses sentiments*

Knowing how to say what you feel is very important in friendships. You need to be honest with your friends, because

friendships are based on trust. You don't need to say a lot, but you do need to make an effort to say what you feel.

Your French friends feel the same things you do—happy, interested, and confident most of the time, sad and frustrated occasionally. But they explain how they feel in a way that's very different from how you express it. They use a sort of double pronoun. So instead of "I feel great!" your friends say something like, "I, me, feel great!"

Reflexive Pronouns— Pronoms réfléchis

You know when you go to a doctor for a checkup, sometimes he or she tests your reflexes. You get a little whack with a rubber hammer right below your kneecap, and your leg automatically kicks!

There are some verbs in French that have a reflex, too. They don't kick, but they do need a pronoun. In English, we call these verbs, "reflexive verbs," but in French, they're called *les verbes pronominaux*. You can recognize them because they're always hooked up to a pronoun of some sort. The verb "to feel" is one of these verbs. In French, it's *se sentir*.

To understand how these verbs work, you begin by learning the reflexive pronouns in French. Here they are:

English Pronoun	French Subject Pronoun	French Reflexive Pronoun
I	*je*	*me*
you	*tu*	*te*
he/she/it	*il/elle/il*	*se*
we	*nous*	*nous*
you	*vous*	*vous*
they	*ils/elles*	*se*

The reflexive pronouns are a little odd, aren't they? The French reflexive pronoun for "he/she/it" and "they" is the

same, *se*. And the subject pronouns, *nous* and *vous*, are the same as the reflexive pronouns, *nous* and *vous*. Only the *je* and *tu* change to *me* and *te*.

But that's the fun thing about learning a new language—it's full of surprises!

I Feel Good—*Je me sens bien!*

To say how you feel in French, you need the verb *se sentir*. Here is the conjugation map with the reflexive pronouns:

English	French
to feel	*se sentir*
I feel	*je me sens*
you feel	*tu te sens*
he/she/it feels	*il/elle/il se sent*
we feel	*nous nous sentons*
you feel	*vous vous sentez*
they feel	*ils/elles se sentent*

There are several common reflexive verbs in French. They include *se laver* ("to wash"), *se lever* ("to get up"), and *se souvenir* ("to remember").

They all follow the same pattern. The subject, the reflexive pronoun and verb all match.

If, for example, you want to say "I feel good," in French, you say, *Je me sens bien*. And if you say "They feel good," you say, "*Ils se sentent bien!*"

Respecting My Friends—
Respecter ses amis

Getting along well with your French friends is like getting along well with friends from every other country. Most of the time, you just have fun and enjoy each other's company. Sometimes, though, you feel badly and want to express that.

MISTAKES TO AVOID
Fautes à éviter

The reflexive pronouns are very important in French. If you leave them out, you may say something very different from what you intended. If you say, *Je me sens super*, you say, "I feel great!" But if you say, *Je sens super*, you're saying, "I smell great!"

Whole Hearted

Paris is known as "The City of Love," so that means some hearts might get broken. Can you put these back together? Draw a line connecting the proper halves to each other.

When your friends tell you how they feel, you need to listen.

Here's a list of some ways you might feel:

English	French
comfortable	*à l'aise (faux ami)*
uncomfortable	*mal à l'aise*
frustrated	*frustré*
angry	*fâché*
hurt	*blessé*
sad	*triste*
sorry	*désolé*
helpful	*utile*
hopeful	*plein d'espoir*
cheerful	*gai*
confident	*sûr de lui, d'elle*
happy	*heureux*

How Does Your Friend Feel?— *Comment se sent ton ami?*

To say "he feels cheerful" or "we are happy" is easy in English, because you don't have to match all the words like you do in French. But French kids don't have any trouble matching up all the words. From the time they learned to speak, they could say, *Elle se sent heureuse* ("She feels happy"), or *Nous nous sentons heureux* ("We feel happy") without any problem.

Since you're getting the hang of adjectives in French, it's not going to be difficult for you, either! Most of the time, the feminine words get an extra "e" and plural words get an "s." The plural feminine words often get both—

"es." But some words don't need so much fuss to match. Study this map:

M Singular	F Singular	M and F Plural	F Plural
confortable	confortable	confortables	confortables
inconfortable	inconfortable	inconfortables	inconfortables
frustré	frustrée	frustrés	frustrées
fâché	fâchée	fâchés	fâchées
blessé	blessée	blessés	blessées
triste	triste	tristes	tristes
désolé	désolée	désolés	désolées
utile	utile	utiles	utiles
gai	gaie	gais	gaies
confiant	confiante	confiants	confiantes
heureux	heureuse	heureux	heureuses

Using Your Adjectives—*Utiliser tes adjectifs*

As you can see from the map you looked at, if the adjective ends in an "*e*," like *triste* and *utile*, it often doesn't get an extra "*e*" in the feminine words. But if it ends with "*é*," like *fâché*, it often does get that extra "*e*." And the adjectives that end in "x" don't change for singular and plural masculine words, but get a "*se*" for the singular feminine word, and an "*ses*" for the plural feminine word.

Time to practice your adjectives. Next to each description, write the correct form of the French adjective. For example, the answer for "Frustrated, girl, singular" is *frustrée*:

1. Helpful, boy, plural (boys and girls) _____

2. Uncomfortable, girl, plural _____

3. Hurt, boy, singular _____

4. Cheerful, girl, singular _____

5. Sorry, boy, plural _____

6. Sad, girl, plural _____

7. Happy, boy, singular _____

8. Confident, boy, plural (boys and girls) _____

Solving Problems—*Régler des problèmes*

Sometimes even the best of friends have misunderstandings. In French, a "misunderstanding" is a *malentendu*. The word *malentendu* literally means *mal* (bad) + *entendu* (hearing), so when you have a misunderstanding in French, it means you probably haven't listened to each other closely enough. In fact, hearing and understanding are so closely linked, *entendu* means both.

Let's see what you and your friends want to say, so we understand what the problem is. Look at the following sentences and fill in the missing words. Remember how to use your reflexive verbs and pronouns and your adjectives. Pay attention to how all the words match up!

1. *Il _____ sent faché.*

2. *Vous _____ sentez sûrs de vous.*

3. *Nous _____ sentons blessés.*

4. *Je me _____ triste.*

5. *Tu _____ sens gaie.*

6. *_____ se sentent utiles.*

7. *Ils se _____ heureux.*

8. *_____ me sens à l'aise.*

Accidents—*Accidents*

Sometimes friends do something by "accident." It's the same word in French, *un accident*. You don't mean to do something, it just happens because of bad luck or because someone wasn't paying attention. You could slip, for example, and knock someone down by accident. Or a friend could take your coat by mistake.

On the following lines, write a list in English of things that might happen accidentally:

_____

_____

_____

_____

Saying You're Sorry—*Dire que tu es désolé*

Your French friends, just like all your other friends, like to feel that others care about them. You show you care by asking what the problem is and trying to understand. In fact, you have to know what's wrong before you can help make it right! Here are some questions that you might find useful:

English	French
What happened?	*Qu'est-ce qui s'est passé?*
What just happened?	*Qu'est-ce qu'il vient d'arriver ?*
Are you alright?	*Tu n'as rien?*
Are you okay?	*Ça va?*
Can I help you?	*Est-ce que je peux t'aider?*
Can you tell me what's wrong?	*Dis-moi ce qui ne va pas.*
Do you want to talk about it?	*Veux-tu en parler?*

IMPORTANT TIPS
TRUCS IMPORTANTS

When you hurt yourself in French, you don't get a "boo-boo," you get a *bobo*. And when you yell "ouch" in French, you yell *aie*! And instead of going "boom" when you hit the ground, in French you go, *boinks*.

Now let's practice our questions! Look at the following situations described in English, and choose something you might say from the previous list to make your friend feel better. Write what you'd say in French. Since there's more than one way you can ask, try to use as many as possible:

Someone who is crying. _____

Someone who is holding a hurt finger. _____

Someone who fell. _____

Someone who tripped over a step. _____

Someone who is all alone during playtime.

_____

Someone who looks mad. _____

Making Up—*Se réconcilier*

Sometimes when friends have misunderstandings, or when they have an accident, they just want to hear three little words: "I am sorry." In French, you say, *Je suis désolé*. But in some situations, you need to say a little more. You need to say you didn't mean to step on someone's foot! Or that you ate their cake by mistake!

Here are some phrases you might find useful:

English	French
Sorry!	*Désolé!*
Excuse me.	*Pardon.*
I did something wrong.	*Je m'excuse.*
I feel bad about it.	*Je le regrette.*
Let me help you.	*Je vais t'aider.*
I didn't do it on purpose.	*Je ne l'ai pas fait exprès.*

I made a mistake. *Je me suis trompé.*
I misunderstood. *Je n'ai pas compris.*

Say "Sorry" Properly—*Dis "désolé" comme il faut*

Knowing when and how to use "I'm sorry" phrases takes some practice. You don't want to overdo it! But you want to show that you have concern for others. Generally speaking, if the problem is a little one that will be forgotten quickly, a quick *desolé* will often do the trick.

Désolé is good if you accidentally take someone's coat when leaving a party. But if it's an even smaller incident, like bumping into someone in a crowded store, *pardon!* is often all you need.

Look at these sentences and briefly describe (in English) a situation in which you might say them. Try to come up with a different situation for each phrase:

Je ne l'ai pas fais exprès. _____

Je n'ai pas compris. _____

Je le regrette. _____

Je vais t'aider. _____

Désolé! _____

Je me suis trompé/trompée. _____

Pardon. _____

Je m'excuse. _____

Saying, "It's Okay"—*Dire, "Ça va."*

When it's time to forget about a misunderstanding or an accident, you usually say, "It's okay," in English. Or you might say, "Forget about it." Or even just "Not a problem." Often in

---

MISTAKES TO AVOID
Fautes à éviter

Don't forget to say you're sorry when you've hurt someone, even accidentally. Don't worry if it feels strange to speak in French. If you don't say what you want to say correctly, the fact that you cared will still come through.

Negative sentences in French often are reduced to a couple of words. *Ce n'est pas grave* ("It's not serious") sounds like *pas grave*, and *Ce n'est pas un problème* ("It's not a problem") sounds like *pas de problème*.

situations like these, your French friends don't speak in complete sentences, but the meaning is still understood.

Here are some phrases you might want to know:

English	French
Not a problem.	*Pas de problème.*
It's not serious.	*Pas grave.*
It's not a big deal.	*Pas grand chose.*
Forget it.	*Laisse tomber.*
Let me help you.	*Je vais t'aider.*
I didn't do it on purpose.	*Je ne l'ai pas fait exprès.*
I made a mistake.	*Je me suis trompé.*
Let's forget about it.	*On oublie.*
It's over!	*Fini!*

Let's put together all the words you'll need to excuse yourself in case of a misunderstanding. Look at the English language clues and write what you might say in French in the lines that follow. Since there's more than one response in French, try to use as many as you can:

You want to shake hands like a good sport. _____

You feel a little annoyed, but not angry. _____

You want to admit you made a mistake. _____

You didn't do it on purpose. _____

You want to just forget about it. _____

You don't think it's worth any more attention. _____

Girlfriends and Boyfriends— *Amoureux et amoureuses*

When French kids like other kids in a special way, they use the words *amoureux* ("boyfriend") and *amoureuse* ("girlfriend"). They also use a verb you already know, *aimer* ("to like" or "to love"). But *aimer* gets a bit tricky!

To Like a Lot—*Aimer bien*

Remember the different pronouns you've learned so far? You've learned the subject pronouns (*je, tu, il/elle/il, nous, vous, ils/elles*) and the reflexive pronouns (*me, te, se, nous, vous, se*). *Aimer* uses yet another kind of pronoun. Not the subject one, and not the reflexive one, though they're sort of the same. It's something called the "direct object" pronoun. Take a look at the map:

English Pronoun	French Subject Pronoun	French Direct-Object Pronoun
I	*je*	*me*
you	*tu*	*te*
he/she/it	*il/elle/il*	*le/la*
we	*nous*	*nous*
you	*vous*	*vous*
they	*ils/elles*	*les*

> ## IMPORTANT TIPS
> ### TRUCS IMPORTANTS
> Remember to use contractions with your pronouns when they precede a verb that begins with a vowel. *Je le aime* will really confuse your French friends. The correct way of saying it is *Je l'aime*.

Je l'aime

Make some hearts for someone you love...
or just like a lot!

1. Fold paper three times, always in the same direction. If you are folding lengthwise, continue that way

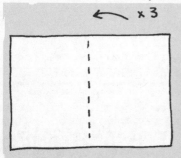

2. Draw a heart with a stand to put it on. Make sure the inside of the heart is on the fold.

3. Cut from the outside (not the fold) along the line of your drawing.

4. Unfold and color. You can write messages on the hearts, too!

Direct Object Pronouns— *Les Pronoms objet directs*

Here's how your new pronoun works. You know how in English, you say, "I love him"? You use a formula like this: Subject + verb + object. You use the same formula when you talk about your friends, "He loves her."

In French, the same information is in the sentence, but it's laid out in a different way. The formula looks like this: Subject + object + verb. So "I love him" is *Je* + *le* + *aime* = *Je l'aime*.

And "He loves her" is *Il l'aime*.

But if you just want to say, "I like her a lot," instead of "I love her," you use the same formula, but you add *bien* after the verb. It looks like this: *Je l'aime bien*. And if he likes her a lot, it's *Il l'aime bien*.

Let's see how you do. Translate each English sentence into French. If you need help remembering the French conjugation map for *aimer*, turn back to Chapter 2.

1. She loves him. _____

2. She likes him a lot. _____

3. We love her. _____

4. You love her. _____

5. She loves you. _____

6. He loves them. _____

7. He likes you a lot. _____

8. You like her a lot. _____

Now you're ready to say nice things to your French friends and learn to understand each other, too.

English-French Dictionary

English	French	English	French	English	French
active	*actif/active*	coin	*une pièce*	he	*il*
airplane	*un avion*	computer	*un ordinateur*	healthy	*en bonne santé*
angry	*fâché*	country	*la campagne/le pays*	helpful	*utile*
April	*avril*	confident	*sûr de lui*	hi	*salut*
arena	*une arène*	content	*content/contente*	history	*une histoire*
artist	*un/une artiste*	curious	*curieux/curieuse*	holiday	*une fête*
ask	*demander*	cup	*une tasse*	hopeful	*plein d'espoir*
athletic	*sportif/sportive*	dance	*une danse*	house	*une maison*
August	*août*	day	*un jour*	horse riding	*faire du cheval*
bakery	*une boulangerie*	desk	*un bureau*	hurt	*blessé*
ball	*un ballon*	department	*le grand*	I	*Je*
bathroom	*les toilettes/la salle de bains*	store	*magasin*	January	*janvier*
		doctor	*un docteur*	June	*juin*
be	*être*	dog	*un chien*	July	*juillet*
beach	*une plage*	earth	*la Terre*	know	*savoir*
bedroom	*une chambre à cou cher*	easy-going	*décontracté*	lazy	*paresseux/paresseuse*
		eat	*manger*	library	*une bibliothèque*
big	*gros/grosse*	English	*l'anglais*	like	*aimer*
bike	*un vélo*	excited	*enthousiaste, content de*	live	*vivre*
bill	*un billet*			literature	*littérature*
bird	*un oiseau*	eyes	*les yeux*	love	*aimer*
birthday	*un anniversaire*	February	*février*	magic	*une magie*
black	*noir*	ferry	*un ferry*	map	*une carte*
blue	*bleu*	finished	*fini*	mathematics	*les mathématiques*
boat	*un bateau*	fish	*un poisson*	May	*mai*
body	*un corps*	flower	*une fleur*	March	*mars*
bookstore	*une librairie*	Friday	*vendredi*	midnight	*minuit*
boy	*un garçon*	friend	*ami/amie, copain/copine*	mistake	*une faute*
brown	*marron*			Mom	*une maman*
bus	*un bus*	friendly	*sympa*	Monday	*lundi*
buy	*acheter*	frog	*une grenouille*	month	*un mois*
call	*appeler*	frustrated	*frustré*	morning	*le matin*
car	*une voiture*	funny	*drôle*	movie store	*un magasin de film*
cat	*un chat*	games	*jeux*	music	*une musique*
change	*la monnaie*	girl	*une fille*	name	*un nom*
cheerful	*gai*	give back	*rendre*	nice	*gentil/gentille*
chess	*les échecs*	green	*vert*	night	*la nuit*
city	*une ville*	generous	*généreux/généreuse*	no	*non*
clock	*une horloge*	grocery store	*une épicerie*	noon	*midi*
color	*une couleur*	hair	*les cheveux*	November	*novembre*
comfortable	*confortable (pour un fauteuil)*	happy	*heureux/heureuse*		

English	French
numbers	les chiffres
October	octobre
OK	d'accord
personality	le caractère
place	un endroit
play	jouer
photographs	les photos
physical education	l'éducation physique
please	s'il te plaît/s'il vous plaît
purple	violet
put	mettre
reading	la lecture
relaxed	détendu
repeat	répéter
red	rouge
restaurant	un restaurant
sad	triste
Saturday	samedi
school	une école
science	les sciences
September	septembre
serious	sérieux/sérieuse
sensitive	sensible
she	elle
shy	timide
singing	le chant
skinny	maigre
small	petit
snake	un serpent
soccer	foot
sorry	désolé/pardon
Spanish	l'espagnol
speak	parler
spelling	l'orthographe
spring	le printemps
social studies	la sociologie
star	une étoile
step-mother	une belle-mère
store	un magasin

English	French
stubborn	têtu/têtue
suburb	la banlieue
subway	un métro
summer	l'été
Sunday	dimanche
take	prendre
tall	grand/grande
teacher	professeur/instituteur
tell	dire
tennis	le tennis
thank you	merci
thin	mince
thing	un truc/une chose
they	ils/elles
Thursday	jeudi
tired	fatigué/fatiguée
today	aujourd'hui
tomorrow	demain
tour bus	un autocar
toy store	un magasin de jouets
translate	traduire
train	un train
Tuesday	mardi
uncomfortable	inconfortable (une chaise)/Mal à l'aise
understand	comprendre
volleyball	le volleyball
wait	attendre
want	vouloir
Wednesday	mercredi
we	nous/on
week	une semaine
what	quoi, quel, quelle
when	quand
where	où
white	blanc
winter	l'hiver
woman	une femme, une dame (lady)
word	un mot
writing/to write	l'écriture/écrire
yellow	jaune

English	French
yes	oui
yesterday	hier
year	une année
you	tu/vous

accents
Marks that go above and below letters to indicate pronunciation. "é" and "ç" are examples of letters with accents.

article
A small word, like "a" or "the," used in front of a noun.

contraction
A short way of putting words together. In English, "they are" is contracted to "they're." In French, *j'aime* is a contraction of *je* and *aime*.

command
A sentence that tells someone to do something. "Stop!" and "Wait!" are examples of commands.

complement
Usually the words at the end of a sentence. In "I go to the store," the phrase "to the store" is a complement. Often complements are described as being "direct objects" and "indirect objects."

conjugation
Changing a verb ending so that it matches with the subject. In "She walks," there is an "s" at the end of the verb "walk." But there is no "s" on the same verb when it is used with other pronouns. "I walk," and "You walk," for example, don't have an "s."

conjugation map
A chart showing how the verb changes to match with the subject.

direct object
The thing that receives the action of the verb. In "I eat cherries," the word "cherries" is the direct object.

gender
Describes whether a word is masculine or feminine. *Le livre*, for example, is a masculine word in French, but *la chaise* is a feminine word.

grammar
The rules of a language. If we want to make a plural in English, for example, we often add an "s" to the noun, so that "dog" becomes "dogs."

linking word
A word that links two parts of a sentence. "Of" is a linking word.

noun
A person, place or thing word. "Jeanette," "cat," and "village" are all nouns.

partitive article
A kind of linking word that says "some." In French, to say "I want some water," you have to use partitive article, *Je veux de l'eau.*

pronunciation
How a word sounds when it's spoken. Every time you speak, you are pronouncing the words.

proper nouns
Specific names of people and places. *Laurent* and *Paris* are examples of proper nouns.

plural
When a word refers to more than one thing. "Cats" is an example, because there is more than one cat.

pronoun
A word that substitutes for a noun. "He" and "she" are examples of pronouns.

reflexive pronouns
Special kinds of pronouns that repeat the subject. In the French sentence, *je me lève*, the reflexive pronoun, *me*, reinforces the subject pronoun, *je*.

sentence formula
A way of putting the parts of a sentence together. "I + go + to the park = I go to the park" is an example of a sentence formula.

singular
When a word refers to one thing. In "a desk," there is only one desk, so "desk" is singular.

subject
The nouns or pronouns in a sentence that the verb talks about. In "He plays music," the word "he" is the subject.

subject pronouns
Pronouns that usually start off a sentence. In English, "he," "we," and "they" are examples of pronouns.

tense
The time the verb talks about. "I am hungry" is in the present tense because it refers to now. "I was hungry" is in the past tense, because it refers to an event in the past.

translation
Changing the words from one language to another but keeping the same meaning. "Thank you" translated into French is *merci*.

verb
The action word in a sentence. In "I bought a new book," the word "bought" is the verb.

Puzzle Answers

page 4 • **Alphabackwards**

Miel - Honey

Kangourou - Kangaroo

Jouet- Toy

Bebe - Baby

Aller - To go

page 10 • **Funny Phone**

trwah _3_ trwah _3_ uh _1_

sank _5_ zayroh _0_ set _7_

weet _8_ weet _8_ duh _2_

duh _2_ nerf _9_

page 26 • **Joyeux Anniversaire**

page 35 • **Excuse-Moi!**

page 43 • **It's You**

Je mange des
fruits

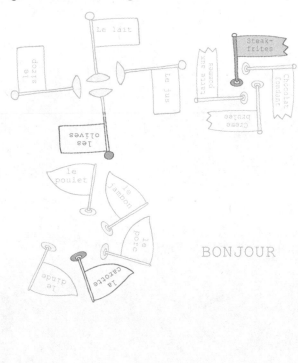

Le lait

le sirop

le jus

tarte aux pommes

Steak-frites

Chocolat fondant

crème brûlée

les olives

le poulet

le jambon

le porc

la dinde

la carotte

BONJOUR

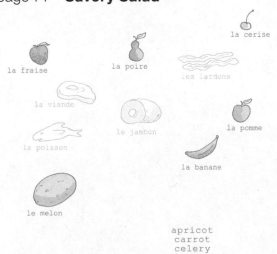

la cerise

la fraise

la poire

les lardons

la viande

le jambon

la pomme

la poisson

la banane

le melon

apricot
carrot
celery
herb
lentil

le coffre-fort   ma poche   la banque

Lucy is going to
la librairie - the
bookstore

mon sac   mon sac-à-dos

mon
portefeuille   mon tiroir

J'ai
  froid

What
season
is it?

l'hiver

J'ai
  chaud

What
season
is it?

l'ete

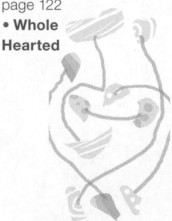

Exercise Answers

Chapter 1
PAGE 9
1. Which French letter sounds similar to the "a" in "Dad"? *à*
2. Which French letters sound like the "sh" in "ship"? *ch*
3. Which French letters sound like "oo" in "boot"? *ou*
4. Which French letter is often silent? *h*

PAGE 14
1. I eat   *Je mange*
2. We give back   *Nous rendons*
3. *Vous mangez*   You eat
4. *Tu finis*   You finish

Chapter 2
PAGE 19
1. 9:10 A.M.   *neuf heures dix*
2. 2:15 A.M.   *deux heures quinze*
3. 4:45 A.M.   *cinq heures moins le quart*
4. 5:30 P.M.   *dix-sept heures et demie*
5. 12:30 A.M.   *minuit et demi*
6. 11:25 P.M.   *vingt-trois heures vingt-cinq*
7. 1:48 A.M   *une heure quarante-huit*
8. 2:20 P.M.   *quatorze heures vingt*

PAGE 21
1. *le dix juin mille huit cent quatre-vingt douze?* 10 juin 1892
2. *le quatre juillet mille sept cent treize?* 4 juillet 1713
3. *le treize février mille cinq cent dix-sept?* 13 février 1517
4. *le vingt-sept mai mille neuf-cent soixante-et-un?* 27 mai 1961

Chapter 4
PAGE 44
1. Your best friend   *Tu*
2. Your teachers   *Vous*
3. Your mom   *Tu*
4. A bus driver   *Vous*
5. A kid your age you meet on the playground   *Tu*
6. Your friend's dad   *Vous*
7. Your doctor   *Vous*
8. Two police officers   *Vous*

PAGE 52
1. *Peux-tu venir demain?   Je peux venir demain.*
2. *Veux-tu venir chez moi?   Oui, je veux venir chez toi.*
3. *Peux-tu demander à ta mère?   Je vais demander à ma mère.*
4. *Peux-tu venir aujourd'hui?   Je peux venir aujourd'hui.*
5. *Peux-tu dormir chez moi?   Je peux dormir chez toi.*
6. *Peux-tu venir après l'école?   Je peux venir après lécole.*

Chapter 5
PAGE 61
1. a climbing structure   *une cage à écureuil*
2. the merry-go-round/the carousel   *le tourniquet, le manège*
3. some swings   *des balançoires*
4. the basketball court   *le terrain de basket*
5. the roller skates   *les rollers*
6. some slides   *des toboggans*
7. the soccer field   *le terrain de foot*
8. some tunnels   *des tunnels*

PAGE 64
1. *Tu aimes faire de l'équitation.   Vous aimez faire de l'équitation.*
2. *Tu veux faire du ski.   Vous voulez faire du ski.*
3. *Tu veux faire des courses de vélo.   Vous voulez faire des courses de vélo.*
4. *Tu aimes faire de l'escrime.   Vous aimez faire de l'escrime.*
5. *Tu aimes faire du golf.   Vous aimez faire du golf.*
6. *Tu aimes faire du tir à l'arc.   Vous aimez faire du tir à l'arc.*

PAGE 66
1. *Lance!   Tu*
2. *Gagnez!   Vous*
3. *Attendez!   Vous*
4. *Attrape!   Tu*
5. *Frappez!   Vous*
6. *Arrête!   Tu*

Chapter 6
PAGE 77
1. *Il mange du broccoli.*   He eats broccoli.
2. *Elles boivent de l'eau.*   They drink water.
3. *Nous buvons du vin.*   We drink wine.
4. *Je mange des carottes.*   I eat carrots.
5. *Tu bois du jus.*   You drink juice.
6. *Il boit du sirop.*   He drinks soft drinks.
7. *Vous mangez des cerises.*   You eat cherries.
8. *Ils mangent du poulet.*   They eat chicken.

PAGE 78
1. *Tu manges du yaourt.   Tu ne manges pas de yaourt.*
2. *Elle boit du coca.   Elle ne boit pas de coca.*
3. *Vous mangez du beurre.   Vous ne mangez pas de beurre.*
4. *Ils mangent du porc.   Ils ne mangent pas de porc.*
5. *Nous mangeons des pommes.   Nous ne mangeons pas de pommes.*
6. *Je bois de la citronnade.   Je ne bois pas de citronnade.*
7. *Je mange de la dinde.   Je ne mange pas de dinde.*
8. *Tu manges des cerises.   Tu ne manges pas de cerises.*

Chapter 7

PAGE 85

1. *Elles prennent un avion.* Elles vont prendre un avion.
2. *Il prend le bateau.* Il va prendre le bateau.
3. *Nous prenons une voiture.* Nous allons prendre une voiture.
4. *Je prends le bus.* Je vais prendre le bus.
5. *Vous prenez un ferry.* Vous allez prendre un ferry.
6. *Tu prends l'autocar.* Tu vas prendre l'autocar.

PAGE 92

1. *Elles viennent de mettre un billet dans un tiroir.*
2. *Il vient de mettre son argent dans son sac-à-dos.*
3. *Nous venons de mettre nos Euros dans un sac.*
4. *Je viens de mettre la monnaie dans le portefeuille.*
5. *Vous venez de mettre vos Euros dans un coffre-fort.*
6. *Tu viens de mettre cinquante Euros et trente centimes à la banque.*

PAGE 95

1. *Je le veux plus grand.* I want it bigger.
2. *Nous la voulons plus grande.* We want it bigger.
3. *Tu le veux plus petit.* You want it smaller.
4. *Il la veut plus petite.* He wants it smaller.
5. *Elles veulent le même.* They want the same.
6. *Vous la voulez un petit peu plus grande.* You want it a little bit bigger.
7. *Ils le veulent un petit peu plus petit.* They want it a little bit smaller.

Chapter 8

PAGE 99

1. *Elles sont là, devant les fleurs.* They are there, in front of the flowers.
2. *Nous sommes ici, sur la pelouse.* We are here, on the lawn.
3. *Tu es là, devant l'arbuste.* You are there, in front of the shrub.
4. *Ils sont là-bas, sous le parasol.* They are over there, under the umbrella.
5. *Je suis ici, sur le chemin.* I am here, on the path.
6. *Vous êtes là, derrière la haie.* You are there, behind the hedge.

PAGE 106

1. *J'ai soif.* I am thirsty.
2. *Ils ont chaud.* They are hot.
3. *Elles ont faim.* They are hungry.
4. *Elle a faim.* She is hungry.
5. *Elle a froid.* She is cold.
6. *Nous avons chaud.* We are hot.
7. *Vous avez froid.* You are cold.
8. *J'ai sommeil.* I am sleepy.

PAGE 111

1. *J'ai vu un zèbre.*
2. *Nous avons vu une girafe.*
3. *Elles ont vu un éléphant.*
4. *Il a vu une autruche.*
5. *Tu as vu un tigre.*
6. *Il a vu un ours.*
7. *Ils ont vu un serpent.*
8. *Nous avons vu un crocodile.*

Chapter 9

PAGE 119

1. *Theo est son meilleur ami.*
2. *Noah est son meilleur ami.*
3. *Solène est sa meilleure amie.*
4. *Ebba, Gwen, Lisa et Nikki sont ses meilleures amies.*
5. *Laurent et Philippe sont ses meilleurs amis.*
6. *Jeanette, Philippe et Sally sont ses meilleurs amis.*
7. *Jody et Kiko sont ses meilleurs amis.*
8. *Jeanette est sa meilleure amie.*

PAGE 123

1. Helpful, boy, plural (boys and girls) *utiles*
2. Uncomfortable, girl, plural *inconfortables*
3. Hurt, boy, singular *blessé*
4. Cheerful, girl, singular *gaie*
5. Sorry, boy, plural *désolés*
6. Sad, girl, plural *tristes*
7. Happy, boy, singular *heureux*
8. Confident, boy, plural (boys and girls) *sûrs d'eux*

PAGE 124

1. *Il se sent fâché.*
2. *Vous vous sentez sûrs de vous.*
3. *Nous nous sentons blessés.*
4. *Je me sens triste.*
5. *Tu te sens gaie.*
6. *Ils se sentent utiles.*
7. *Ils se sentent heureux.*
8. *Je me sens à l'aise.*

PAGE 130

1. She loves him. *Elle l'aime.*
2. She likes him a lot. *Elle l'aime bien.*
3. We love her. *Nous l'aimons.*
4. You love her. *Tu l'aimes.*
5. She loves you. *Elle vous aime.*
6. He loves them. *Il les aime.*
7. He likes you a lot. *Il t'aime bien.*
8. You like her a lot. *Tu l'aimes bien.*